CAPITAL CARICATURES

Capital Caricatures

A selection of etchings by

John Kay

SHEILA SZATKOWSKI

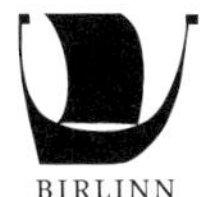

BIRLINN

First published in 2007 by
Birlinn Limited
West Newington House
10 Newington Road
Edinburgh
EH9 1QS

www.birlinn.co.uk

ISBN 13: 978 1 84158 658 8
ISBN 10: 1 84158 658 7

British Library Cataloguing-in-Publication Data
A catalogue record for this book is available
from the British Library

Design by James Hutcheson and Mark Blackadder

Typset in Monotype Bell

Printed and bound in Poland
Produced by Polskabook

FOR JOSEF SZATKOWSKI

and with thanks to
all who have helped preserve
the memory of John Kay

Contents

CONTENTS

Foreword

Great cities have their distinctive moments, and the artists to record those moments. The London of Thomas Rowlandson, the Paris of Toulouse-Lautrec and the Berlin of George Grosz are all examples of cities which found just the right artist to record a particular period of their life. Edinburgh, although smaller than these three, was for a brief and glorious spell in the eighteenth century the intellectual capital of Europe. Fortunately there were artists to capture that remarkable century in the city's existence, prominent among them being Sir Henry Raeburn, whose portraits of the great men and women of his time provide us with some of the finest paintings of the age. But there was another artist at work in Georgian and Regency Edinburgh, and he was a man of humbler stripe, the barber, John Kay.

From his shop in the Old Town, Kay observed the comings and goings of the citizens of this remarkable city. Many portrait painters record only the features of the rich and the successful: to sit for Raeburn would require fifty guineas or so, a fortune for most. Kay, by contrast, drew the lowest and the highest, as a sort of indiscriminate, early *paparazzo* – the itinerant beggar and the man of property, the scoundrel and the cleric, the elegant and the grotesque. The whole human comedy is recorded in these pages, lovingly preserved for us in these charming miniatures.

A particularly fascinating aspect of these portraits is the fact that they record the city at a time when its Scottish character was still strong. During the Victorian period Scotland embarked upon the British adventure with gusto, and Edinburgh increasingly saw its destiny as part of a growing, London-dominated empire. In John Kay's time, however, the memory of the old Scotland was still vivid, and recent, and a distinctive Scottish culture was still very much in evidence. This shines forth in all these pictures – in the craggy independence illuminating many of the faces; in the canniness; in the humour; in habits of dress. These are very Scottish pictures, but they also show the very heart of Edinburgh, the mixture of pride and pawkiness that give the city its special character.

Kay's talents are manifold. He has the true miniaturist's skill of encapsulating a great deal within a very small compass. He has a marvellous eye for detail. His backgrounds are subtle and skilfully complementary. But most of all, he has that wonderful ability to capture in the faces of his subjects a whole world-view. Thus we have the theologians in all their rectitude, the military men in all their strutting splendour, the burgesses of the town in all their respectability. Every one of these faces tells us something about the society of Kay's time.

All of which you will see when you open the pages of this book and look upon the engravings. But there is something more. Gaze upon these portraits and then take a walk around the Old Town of Edinburgh and into the New Town. Find a convenient coffee house and contemplate the faces of the passers-by. They are still there – the people whom Kay observed – are still there!

Alexander McCall Smith

Preface

A historian might entertain the idea of being transported back to another era, more often than not to a chosen period for research. For my part, the destination of choice is late eighteenth- and early nineteenth-century Edinburgh, from where I shall observe the comings and goings in Parliament Square, ponder the slow and chequered demise of the old order, and watch in awe as the New Town takes shape, drawing away the professional classes and gentry to the far side of the Nor Loch.

John Kay has offered to play host for my visit and has fulfilled my request to assemble one hundred of my favourite Edinburgh characters for a convivial get-together with claret and oysters at Fortune's Tavern in Old Stamp Office Close. Thanks to this talented artist and all the biographical notes supplied to me by James Paterson and Hugh Paton, I shall get to know a wonderful cross-section of Edinburgh society: lawyers and literati, soldiers and shopkeepers, Provosts and professors, medics and mendicants. Moreover, I can finally ask him the whereabouts of the six hundred or so missing etchings.

You are welcome to join me forthwith.

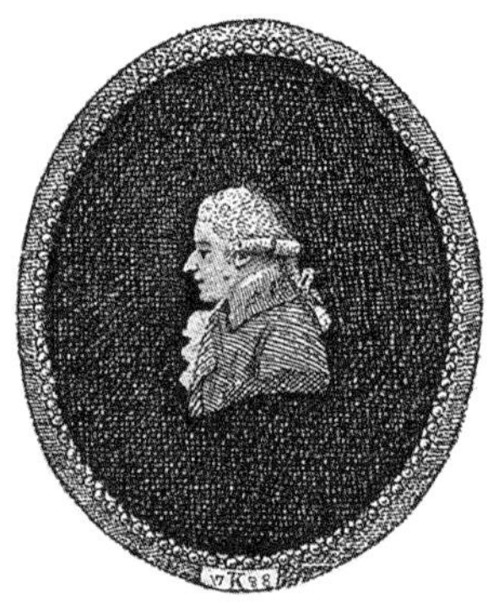

John Kay (1742–1826)

Passed over too often by art critics yet adored by historians, John Kay has left a perceptive chronicle of a unique period of Edinburgh history.

Kay was born in Dalkeith on 6 April 1742 and settled in Edinburgh as a journeyman barber at the age of nineteen. Having purchased the freedom of the Society of Surgeon-Barbers of Edinburgh on 19 September 1771, he was able to set up shop in the Old Town, first in the High Street and later in Parliament Square, and for a short time in Princes Street. Privacy for wealthy professionals would only come with the building of the New Town but for now Kay could look out of his window at the seething panorama of Edinburgh citizenry who lived and worked side by side within the dense confines of the medieval city. Judges and statesmen trod the same cobbled streets and breathed the same foul air as the fishwives and bailies, while doctors and tradesmen, clergy and literati lived cheek by jowl. None could keep secrets in a town where the focus of social life was the tavern or the coffee house.

In his spare time Kay drew exact and faithful likenesses of those around him as well as recording incidents that would amuse the locals, and his prints became so popular that he decided in 1785 to give up barbering to open a print shop. He was fortunate in his patron, Sir William Nisbet of Dirleton, with whom he spent much of 1783 and 1784, using the time to execute numerous etchings. On Sir William's death Kay received an annuity of £20 and henceforth supported himself entirely by his etching and by painting miniatures.

While Kay's work was never as savage as Gillray's and Rowlandson's politically motivated sarcasm, many of his more satirical prints were often bought by the subjects themselves so that they could be destroyed. He was cudgelled at least once and prosecuted, albeit unsuccessfully, on another occasion. Like a true satirist Kay drew attention to the human frailties such as vanity, pomposity and greed, but his wit is subtle and even sympathetic to the vilest of subjects, such as Deacon Brodie.

Kay was probably unaware of the great social document that he was creating but he had hopes of publishing his work around 1792 and even prepared a biographical sketch and self-portrait. Despite the abundance of printers and publishers in Edinburgh, the project never took off. However, he did contribute portraits to the annual exhibitions of the Edinburgh Associated Artists from 1811 to 1816, and to the 1822 exhibition of the Institution for the Encouragement of the Fine Arts in Scotland.

He died in Edinburgh on 21 February 1826 and is buried in the northwest corner of Greyfriars Kirkyard. Kay was twice married, first to Lilly Steven, who died in March 1785 and secondly, in 1787, to Margaret Scott, who survived him until her death in November 1835.

After his death the plates were acquired and published by Hugh Paton, a carver and gilder, with biographical notes by James Paterson, under the title *A Series of Original Portraits and Caricature Etchings by the late John Kay, with Biographical Sketches and Illustrative Anecdotes* (Edinburgh, 2 volumes, quarto, 1837–8; octavo edition, 4 volumes, 1842; new quarto edition, with additional plates, 2 volumes, 1877), so rescuing an unparalleled record of the social life and popular habits of Edinburgh in the heyday of the Scottish Enlightenment.

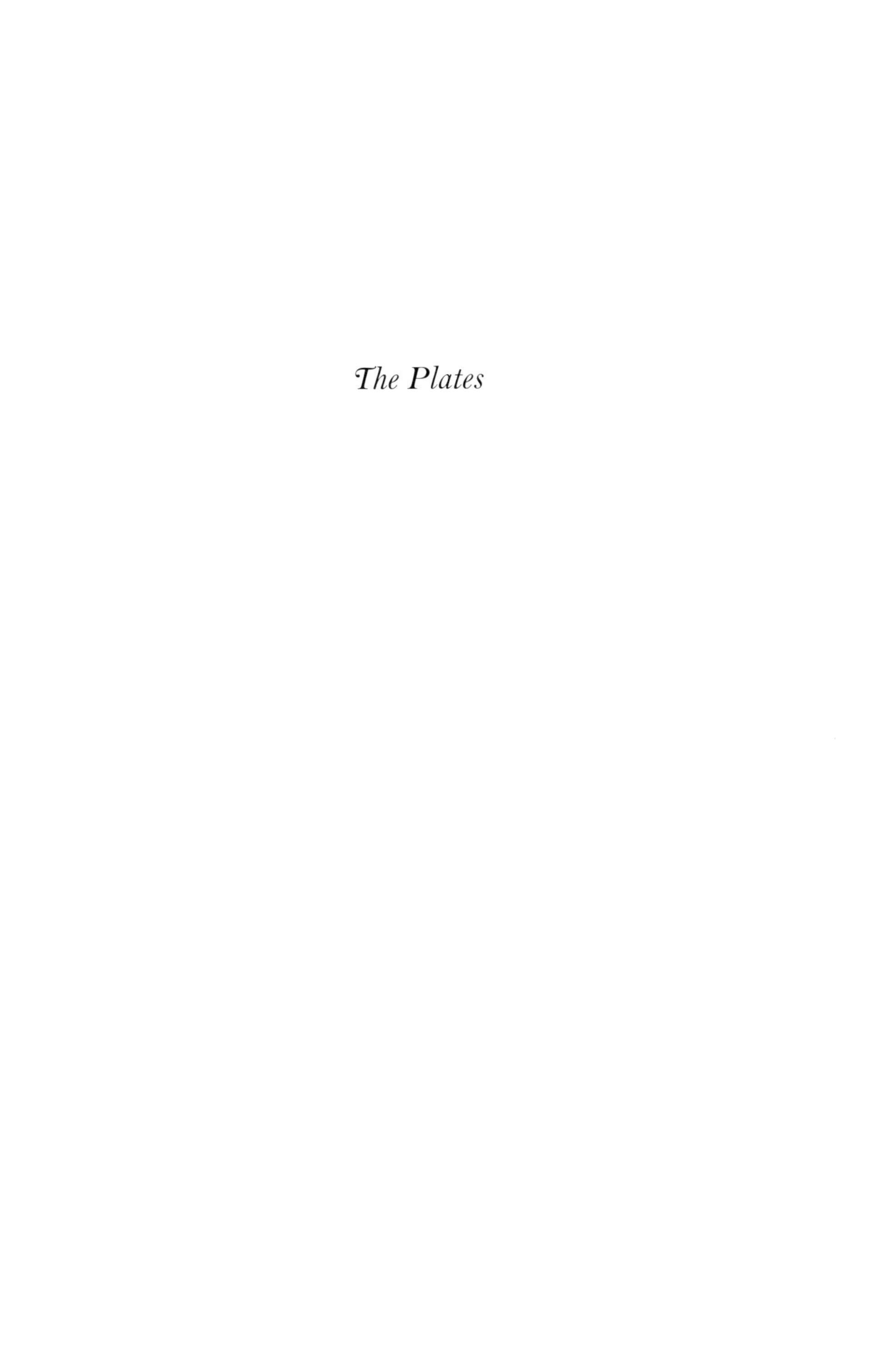

The Plates

Twelve Advocates
Who Plead Without Wigs (1811)

Naked justice for all

Adam Gillies	Lord Newton	James Millar
Sir Walter Scott	Robert Corbet	George Joseph Bell
Wm Rose Robinson	John Wright	John Graham Dalyell
Francis Jeffrey	John Jardine	John Cunninghame

Wearing wigs was a matter of choice for advocates and indicated no distinction in rank. Sir Walter Scott (first in the second row) needs no introduction and Francis Jeffrey (first in the fourth row) is mentioned elsewhere (*LVI*) so it is perhaps worth introducing two lesser-known faces in this popular print.

James Millar (top right) was given the nickname 'Cupid' on account of his ruddy complexion. He was much devoted to the sport of curling and on one occasion when he was due to plead a case before Charles Hay, the first Lord Newton (the second Lord Newton is to the left of Millar in this print), he abandoned the Parliament House to pursue his sport. When the opposing counsel insisted that the case should continue the good-natured judge said 'No, no, the cause may wait until tomorrow, but there is no security that the frost will wait for Mr Millar.'

Sir John Graham Dalyell (last in third row) was one of the first great antiquarians of Scotland. He was the author of numerous works, including the *Early Superstitions of Scotland* and Scott, in the introduction to his 1830 edition of *The Minstrelsy of the Scottish Border*, refers to *Scottish Poems of the Sixteenth Century* (1801) by 'Mr John Grahame Dalzell, to whom his country is obliged for his antiquarian labours'.

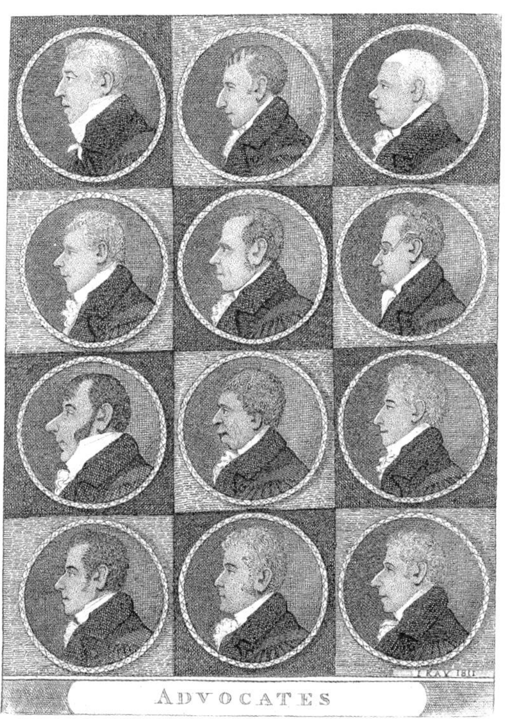

ADVOCATES

Twelve Advocates Who Plead With Wigs On (1810)

Periwigged they prosecute their labours

John Burnett	Robert Bell	Mathew Ross
Edward M'Cormick	George Cranstoun	John Clerk
Sir John Connell	John Hagart	Henry Erskine
Alexander Maconochie	Duncan MacFarlane	Archibald Fletcher (Lord Meadowbank)

Robert Bell, middle of top row, was a son of Benjamin Bell, the eminent surgeon (*V*). He was known for his admiration of the fine arts and belonged to the Bannatyne, Maitland and Abbotsford clubs.

George Cranstoun, middle of the second row, later Lord Corehouse, was a great favourite of Lord Monboddo (*LIX*) who said of him, 'Cranstoun was the only scholar in all of Scotland!' Monboddo considered all other scholars to be south of the Tweed.

The last advocate in this row is John Clerk, later Lord Eldin, who was easily recognised on account of one leg being shorter than the other. Once on hearing a passer-by remark, 'There goes Johnnie Clerk, the lame lawyer', the advocate was quick to retort, 'No, madam; I may be a lame man but I am not a lame lawyer!'

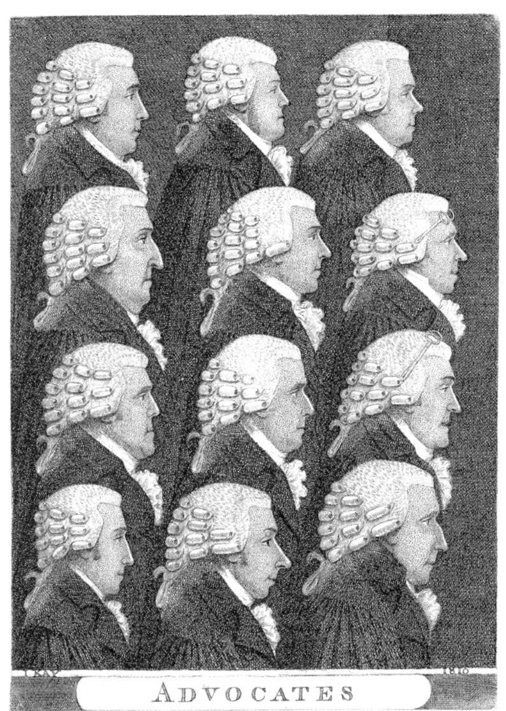

ADVOCATES

A Group of Aeronauts
'Fowls of a Feather Flock Together' (1785)

Taking the aerial view

In Kay's print the celebrated balloonist, Vincent Lunardi (*LXIV*), is placed prominently in the centre and reaching out to shake hands with James Tytler on the left. Although the flamboyant Lunardi delighted spectators with his balloon ascents in Edinburgh in 1785, it is James Tytler who deserves the credit for the first manned aerial ascent in Britain. His Grand Edinburgh Fire Balloon had been exhibited inside the uncompleted dome of Register House before taking off on 27 August 1784 at Comely Gardens, near Holyrood in Edinburgh, and landing half a mile away at Restalrig.

While Lunardi enjoyed celebrity status, James Tytler fared less well, despite his talents as a surgeon and latterly as a writer. He compiled most of the second edition of the *Encyclopaedia Britannica* for a paltry 16 shillings a week, increasing its size from three to eight volumes quarto and managing to omit any reference to the American Revolution. In 1792, having espoused the cause of the Friends of the People, Tytler was the first person in Edinburgh to be detained as part of the government's crackdown on Scotland's radical societies. He fled to the United States, where he died in 1804.

Also noteworthy in this print is John Spottiswood (second from the right to the fore), one of the magistrates of Edinburgh, who took great exception to Kay putting him on a level with the caddy and innkeeper, Myles M'Phail, also known as Lord North on account of the striking resemblance to Lord North, the former Prime Minister.

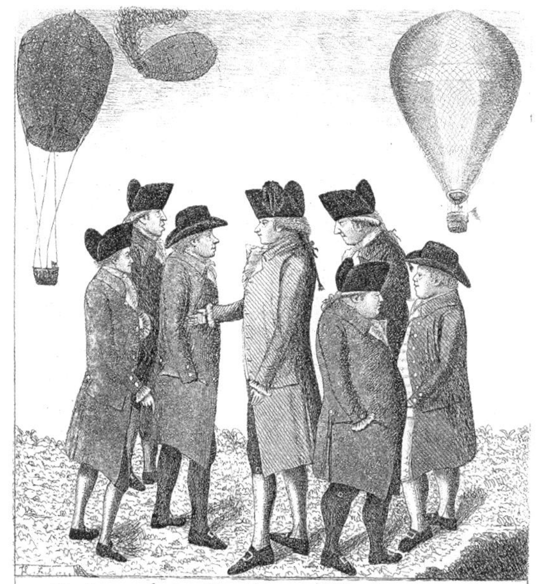

Fowls of a Feather Flock together

Major-General Aytoun
and the Duc d'Angoulême
'The Great and the Small are There' (1797)

A royal view of the awkward squad

'The Great and the Small are There' is the title of Kay's print, a reference to the size and status of the burly General Aytoun alongside the genteel character of the young French duc. It was probably an allusion also to the varied composition of the Volunteers, an 'awkward squad' from all trades and professions who came in all shapes and sizes. Major-General Aytoun was responsible for superintending the drilling of the corps.

The duc, in exile like his father, the Count d'Artois (*XLII*), was a regular attendee at the Saturday drills of the Royal Edinburgh Volunteers, a kind of eighteenth-century *Dad's Army*. The uniform consisted of a dark blue coat with red facings and was very similar to that of the French National Guard. This is perhaps the reason for the exiled Count d'Artois, later Charles X, choosing to stay home at Holyrood, the uniforms being an unwelcome reminder of events back home.

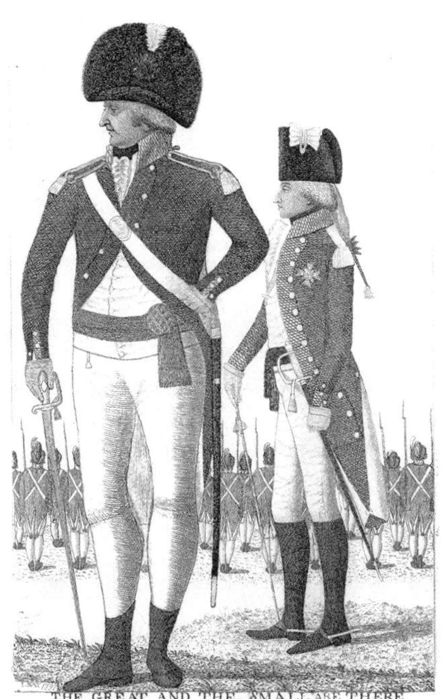

THE GREAT AND THE SMALL ARE THERE

Benjamin Bell, Surgeon (1791)

The assiduous chirugien

Benjamin Bell was one of the best-known surgeons in eighteenth-century Scotland. His *System of Surgery*, published between 1783 and 1788, is considered the first comprehensive textbook on the subject in English and helped secure Edinburgh's international reputation for surgery. Such was the demand for his skills that it was said of him, 'at one time nobody could die contented, without having consulted Benjamin Bell'.

Bell owned extensive lands in Newington, Edinburgh and died there at Newington House in 1806. He was the first of the Bell surgical dynasty. The last of the dynasty was his great-grandson, Sir Joseph Bell, who was used by his pupil Arthur Conan Doyle as the prototype for Sherlock Holmes.

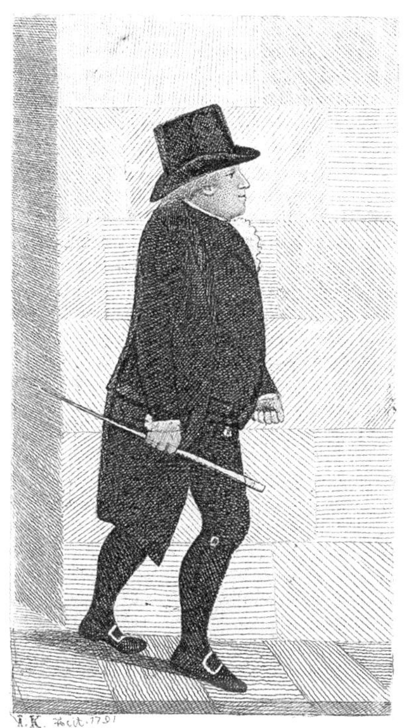

I.K. fecit. 1791

John Bennett, Surgeon (1787)

A gentleman as spare and polished as his scalpel

Kay's etching was deemed to be a very good likeness of John Bennett, right down to the mole on the surgeon's right cheek.

John Bennett trained as a surgeon in Edinburgh and after a period of service with the Sutherland Fencibles, he set up medical practice with James Law in Edinburgh. In 1802 he was elected President of the Royal College of Surgeons of Edinburgh in succession to his partner James Law, the previous incumbent.

With his specialist knowledge of venereal diseases, John Bennett was often called upon to be an expert witness in divorce cases and his testimony proved the downfall of many a wayward spouse. It is interesting to note that Scottish wives, unlike their English counterparts, were able to secure a divorce, with the right to re-marry, if they were able to prove that their husbands were guilty of adultery.

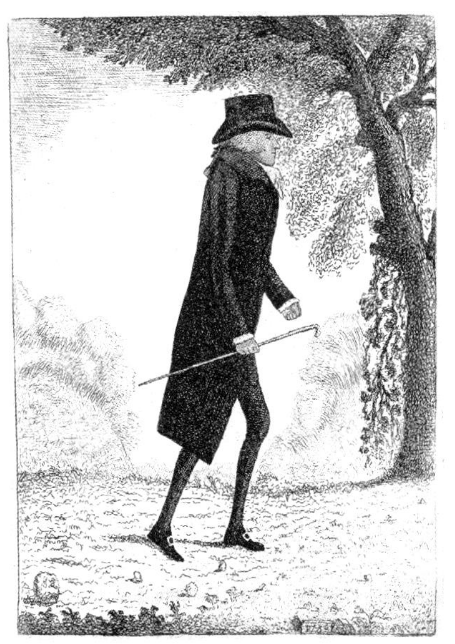

Captain Billair and his wife, who, though a tall woman, always wore high-heeled shoes (1792)

Stepping out in style

In this etching Kay has chosen to accentuate the height difference between Captain Billair and his wife by showing her wearing heels and a very tall hat.

Captain Billair, known as Dickie to his close associates, was a captain in the Rutland Fencible Cavalry, which was commanded by Captain Neville. Quartered in Edinburgh sometime during the year 1792, the Fencibles were really 'de-fencibles' in that they were full-time regulars only during hostilities and were limited to service at home. The Rutland Fencible Cavalry was later renamed the Rutland Light Dragoons.

The captain was known to be very convivial and fond of a 'meridian' or midday drink. He was often invited to private parties and balls but without his wife. According to Kay, the captain's wife did not mind and 'appeared to have philosophy enough to care little for the exclusion'.

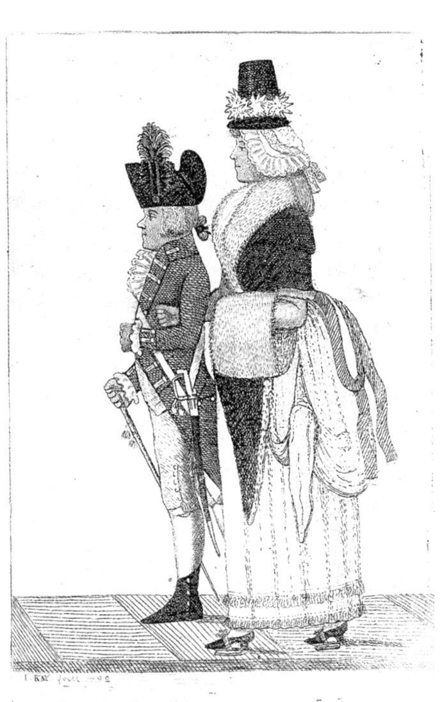

Joseph Black, lecturing (1787)

An enlightened chemist

The eminent scientist and medic is noted for his pioneering work on latent and specific heats and for the discovery of 'fixed air', better known as carbon dioxide. A close associate of Dr William Cullen (*XXIV*), Black left Glasgow in 1766 to succeed him in the chairs of Medicine and Chemistry at Edinburgh.

As well as his 'capital companions', who included Adam Smith (*LXXXVII*), David Hume, Alexander Carlyle and James Hutton (*LV*), Black corresponded extensively on scientific matters with James Watt, whom he had met at Glasgow University. When Watt patented his letter-copying machine in 1780, Black brought Sir William Forbes (*XXXVI*), banker, Adam Smith and Dr William Cullen on board as subscribers, each paying six guineas for the machine and five shillings for the packing box. From 1781 Cullen used the machine to make copies of all his replies to patients and it remained the most important method of copying letters until the advent of the modern typewriter in the late nineteenth century.

Black never married, being a contented and philosophical bachelor all his days. It is said that when he died, he was seated in his chair with a bowl of milk on his knee, and despite breathing his last breath, the bowl remained steady where it had been put.

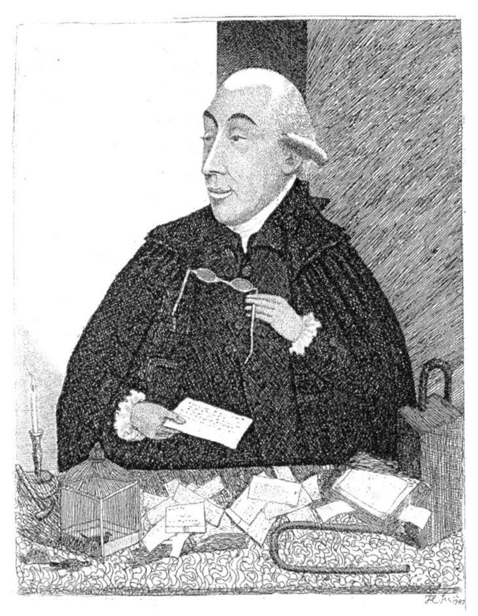

Thomas Blair, late of the Stamp Office, Edinburgh (1792)

The diminutive trencherman

Thomas Blair was appointed Deputy Controller of the Stamp Office in 1784. Short and rotund, he attempted to offset this by wearing a high-crowned cocked hat and having his wig frizzled and powdered and then wired in such a way as to sit an inch higher on his head.

Along with his fellow-workers at the Stamp Office, Blair enjoyed an annual dinner at Fortune's Tavern in Old Stamp Office Close, where his small stature managed to accomplish with ease, 'the demolition of a sirloin' or the 'dissection of a capon'.

He considered himself to have tremendous power of recall and on occasion claimed he could remember his first day on earth, 'I mind the very hour of my birth, and perfectly recollect of my good old mother bidding the midwife close the shutters lest my eyes should hurt with the light!'

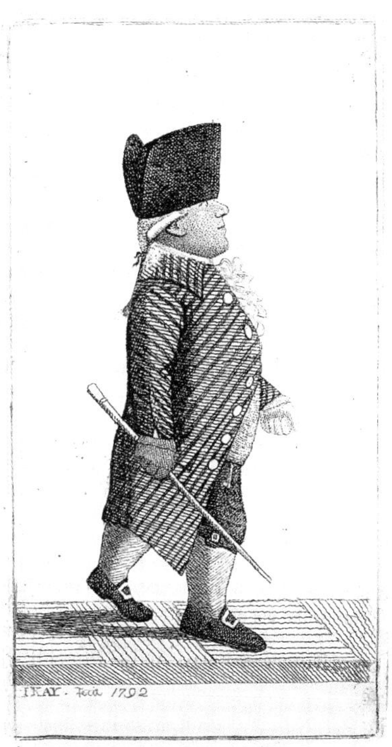
I KAY. Fecit 1792

Neil Fergusson, Advocate
and the Little Polish Count (1802)

A memorable foreign visitor

The print shows Fergusson accompanying the little Polish count, who was three feet three inches in height, to his carriage after a visit to the Parliament House and Advocates Library. The print is dated 1802, several years after the Count's visit in 1788.

Boruwlaski used the title Count Boruwlaski to enhance his commercial appeal in raising funds for himself, but on arrival in Edinburgh in 1788, the visitor's foreign name and diminutive size led to him soon being nicknamed the Count 'Barrel of Whisky'.

Rather than make a demeaning exhibition of himself Boruwlaski chose to 'receive company' for a fee. He stayed in lodgings at 4 St Andrew Street and advertised that he would allow visitors to have breakfast with him at Dun's Hotel in St Andrew Square for three shillings and sixpence. Another option was to visit him at his lodgings for one shilling. For this particular opportunity, the sales proposition, 'Buy now while stocks last' was amended in his advertisement to, 'The Count will positively quit this place on Friday the 7th of August.'

He lived to the ripe old age of ninety-eight and his final resting place in Durham Cathedral is simply marked IB.

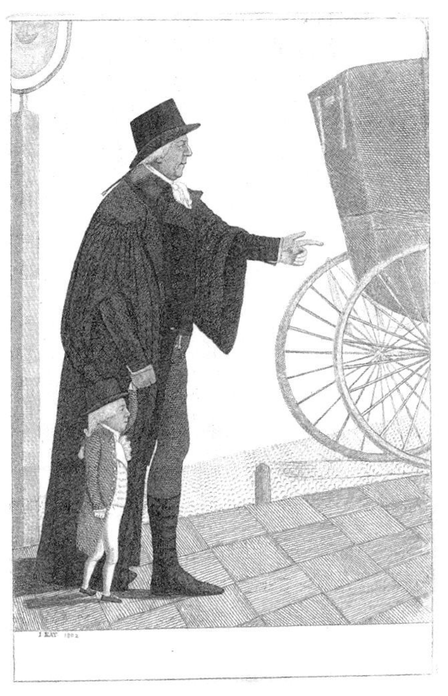

J KAY 1802

Francis Braidwood, Cabinet-maker
'I say, don't laugh, for we are brothers.'
(no date)

Far and sure in the ancient game

The print is intended to be a satire on Braidwood's extravagant dress sense and in particular calls attention to his use of shoelaces, hence the shoelaces on the animals' hoofs. He was not offended by the print but rather joined in the laughter when it appeared.

Braidwood trained as a cabinet-maker in London but returned to Edinburgh where he ran a successful business in the Old Town.

A keen golfer, Braidwood belonged to the Edinburgh Burgess Golfing Club and often took on bets with fellow golfers where he would take two strokes at the ball with a common quart bottle, while his opponents took one stroke with a regular club. He invariably won his bet.

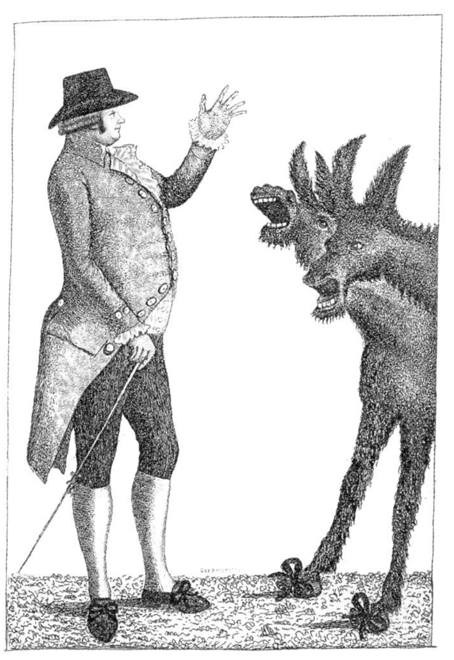

Robert M'Queen of Braxfield, Lord Justice-Clerk (1793)

A jolly hanging judge

Robert M'Queen, Lord Braxfield, the rough diamond of the Edinburgh legal fraternity, was appointed Lord Justice-Clerk in 1788 and presided over several famous trials including those of Deacon Brodie (*LXXXVIII*) and Thomas Muir of Huntershill (*LXXV*).

Well known for his anti-radical comments such as, 'they would a' be muckle the better o' being hanged', Braxfield also mocked his own profession. On one occasion Lord Newton, as a young advocate, was pleading before Braxfield after a night of hard drinking. Braxfield, noting that the opposing counsel was equally befuddled, leant across the bench and announced in broad Scots, 'Gentlemen ye may just pack up your papers and gang hame; the tane o' ye's rifting punch, and the ither's belching claret – and there'll be nae gude got out o' ye the day!'

His direct approach carried over into his personal life, as shown by his proposal of marriage to his second wife, Elizabeth Ord, daughter of Lord Chief Baron Ord. He is said to have addressed her thus, 'Lizzy, I am looking out for a wife, and I thought you just the person that would suit me. Let me have your answer aff or on, the morn, and nae mair about it.' Miss Ord appreciated his style and accepted.

Braxfield is generally regarded to be the model for Lord Hermiston in Stevenson's *Weir of Hermiston* and for all his harsh words and gruff manners, it is claimed that *The Jolly Judge* tavern in Edinburgh's Old Town was named after him.

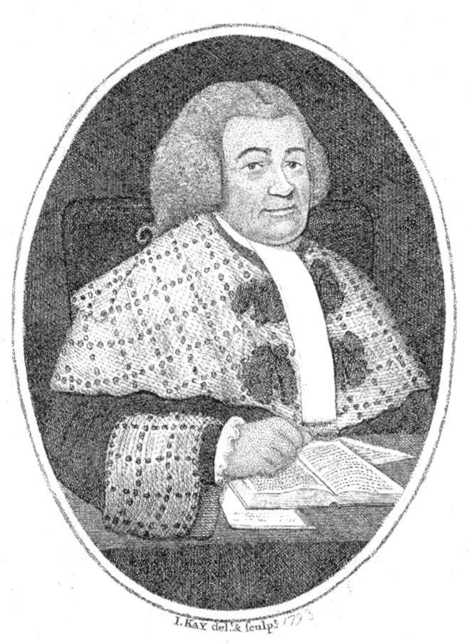

I. KAY del.t & sculpt. 1793

Dr John Brown, Author of
The Brunonian System of Medicine (1786)

An excitable doctor

Dr John Brown is to the fore of the print looking at the ensign of Roman Eagle Lodge, which he founded in 1785. He is also the figure seated to the right of the table with his father-in-law, Mr John Lamont, Mr Little and Lord Bellenden, an accomplished fiddler. Behind them two aspects of the medical fraternity are represented, with the eccentric quack James Graham (*XLVI*) on the left and the intellectuals Dr William Cullen (*XXIV*) and Dr Alexander Hamilton (*L*) in conversation on the right.

A brilliant scholar, Brown gave up theology to study medicine, paying his way by becoming a part-time 'grinder', that is, one who prepared Latin translations of inaugural dissertations for medical students. He became a close associate of Dr William Cullen but friendship turned to rivalry when Brown published his own system of medicine based upon the notion of 'excitability', which was opposed to Cullen's system that assumed the body is maintained in a normal state of health by 'nervous energy'. Brown fled the ensuing storm of controversy in Edinburgh medical circles and went to London, where he died in 1788.

Controversy continued even after Brown's death. His *Elements of Medicine*, revised by Dr Beddoes of Bristol, was published in 1793 and included an interesting engraving of Brown by William Blake. As late as 1802 a two-day riot between Brunonian and non-Brunonian students at the University of Göttingen had to be quelled by a troop of cavalry.

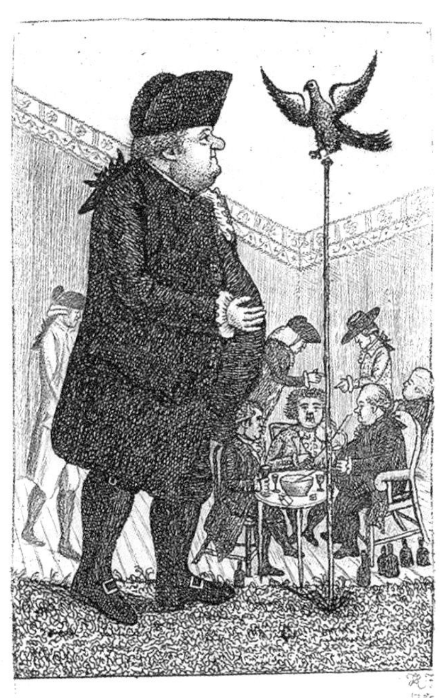

Captain James Burnet,
the Last Captain of the City Guard (1814)

Always up for a wager

The City Guard was first set up in 1696, probably as a political measure, to control any Jacobite disturbances. Acting as a body of armed police, they attended the magistrates at public events and also acted as sentinels at the gates of the city wall. Some were discharged veterans, others were Highlanders, and most were still plying their usual trades and only called out when the occasion required. In 1805 the New Police Bill for Edinburgh came into operation and the City Guard was reduced to a much smaller corps under the captaincy of James Burnet.

Captain James Burnet was known as 'a cheerful companion and an honest man'. When not on duty he was often to be found in a tavern amongst friends. One hot summer's day he took on a wager from James Laing, the Deputy City Clerk, to walk to the top of Arthur's Seat in fifteen minutes. William Smellie (*LXXXVI*) acted as umpire and coach and the determined Captain, who weighed about nineteen stone, reached the summit with thirty seconds to spare but on arrival collapsed 'like an expiring porpoise'. The bet was duly won.

He was also a member of the Lawnmarket Club, a 'dram-drinking, news-mongering, facetious set of citizens' who would make their way each morning to the Post Office for news and then proceed to a tavern for a 'libation of brandy'.

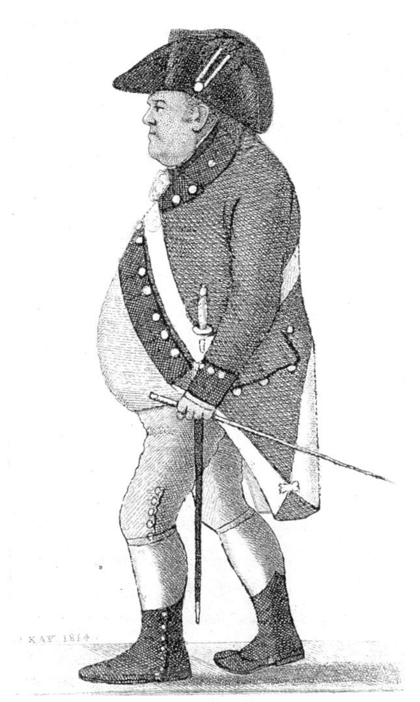

Miss Burns, a Celebrated Beauty (1788)

An endorsement from a namesake

Miss Burns, or Miss Mathews as she was sometimes known, arrived in Edinburgh about the time this print was done by Kay. She soon became known for her beauty and sense of high fashion on the popular evening promenades. However, her neighbours in Rose Street, Edinburgh, reported her for a disturbance and Bailie Creech banished her from the city. The severity of the sentence caused uproar and an appeal was finally granted.

The episode aroused the sympathy of Robert Burns, a namesake but no relation, and he is said to have attributed the following lines to her:

> Cease, ye prudes, your envious railing,
> Lovely Burns has charms – confess;
> True it is, she had one failing –
> Had a woman ever less!

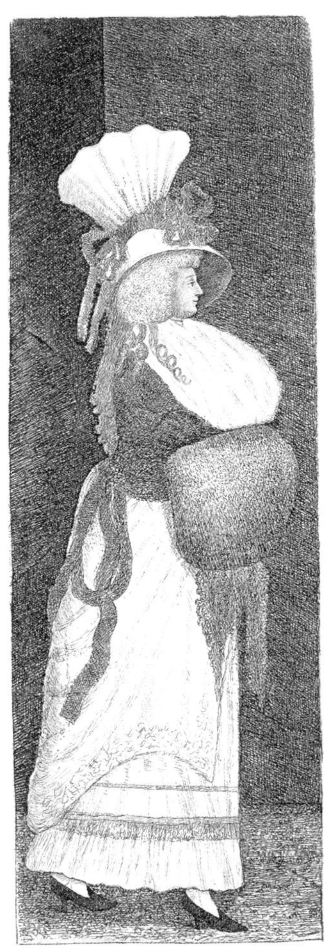

William Butter and
Sir John Morrison (1783)

A social pinch with a poor Knight of Windsor

The print shows William Butter talking to his good friend Sir John Morrison while in the act of taking snuff, often referred to as the 'social pinch'. Butter became a wealthy citizen through expanding his father's cabinet-making business and acquired several properties in Carrubers Close and in Shakespeare Square, which originally stood at the north end of the North Bridge. Besides his business interests, Butter was keen on music and theatre and his father was once heard to comment, 'ne'er an Italian fiddler cam' to Edinburgh but Willie was sure to find him out.'

Sir John Morrison lived in one of Butter's properties in Shakespeare Square. As a young man he had accompanied Charles Douglas, the Earl of Drumlanrig, son of the 3rd Duke of Queensberry, to Lisbon where they witnessed the horrors of the great earthquake of 1755. On his return, Morrison, through the influence of the Queensberry family, obtained a position as Clerk in the Excise Office as well as a place on the roll of the Poor Knights of Windsor, later the Military Knights of Windsor. This body had been set up by Edward III to provide relief and subsistence for brave soldiers in their old age. The Knights were required to pray daily for the Sovereign and Knights Companion of the Order of the Garter and in return they were given a salary and lodgings in Windsor Castle.

For those with a sweet tooth, 'Poor Knights of Windsor' is a colloquial term for French toast.

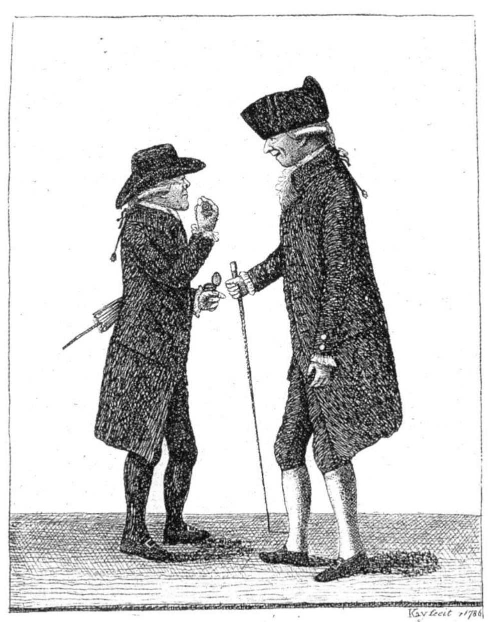

Byrne, the Irish Giant Mr Watson, Mr M'Gowan, Mr Fairholme and Geordie Cranstoun (1784)

A rare specimen comes to town

An early print by Kay, it shows Alexander Watson, a jovial bachelor, talking to Charles Byrne, the Irish giant, with the others listening attentively. Mr Fairholme is the first figure on the left and next to him is John M'Gowan, who lived above Creech the bookseller's shop in the Luckenbooths. On the right, by way of contrast to the giant, is George Cranstoun, the tiny beggar and musician.

Charles Byrne was born in Ireland in 1761 and was known to be over eight feet tall. When he visited Edinburgh in 1784, he shocked locals by lighting his pipe at one of the streetlights on the North Bridge. He also complained of the Auld Reekie chill and a brave Edinburgh tailor took on the job of creating a greatcoat for the giant.

Byrne was a major celebrity in London, where he met the diminutive three feet three inches Count Borulawski (X) in 1782 and aroused the curiosity of John Hunter, the anatomist. Aware of his impending death and determined that his corpse should be kept well away from the reach of 'the chirurgical fraternity' Byrne arranged for his body to be buried at sea. Alas the coffin that his friends dropped into the water contained only stone slabs. It is claimed that the determined Dr Hunter had paid £500 for the corpse to be removed en route while the pallbearers partook of refreshments at a nearby inn. Byrne's skeleton now resides in the Hunterian Museum at the Royal College of Surgeons in London.

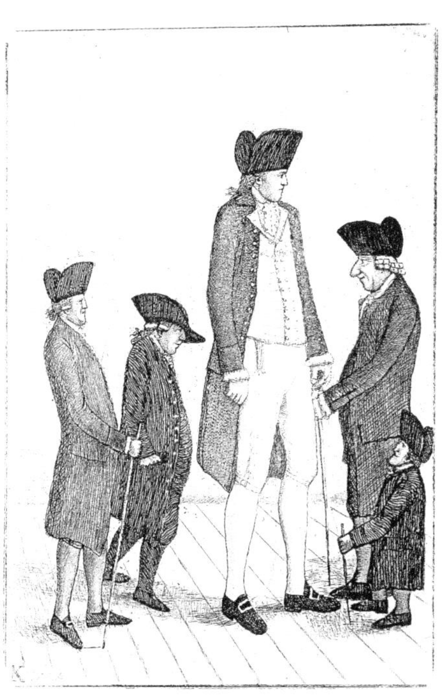

William Pitt and Henry Dundas, afterwards Lord Melville
'The Modern Cain's Lament' (1798)

A friend in need

This is a satirical print directed against William Pitt (*LXXX*) during the hostilities with France. Kay highlights the fragile physique of Pitt with the solid and self-possessed stance of Henry Dundas (*XXXI*), whom he calls 'Harrie'.

Pitt is complaining about the implications of his actions in initiating hostilities towards France:

> O Harrie whether shall I fly! I am this day, A Murderer of thousands, Every one that finds me will count me his Enemy and Slay me.

Dundas was a close friend and steadfast supporter of Pitt the Younger, with his talents gaining him several senior government roles including Treasurer of the Navy (1783–1800) and Secretary for War during the early Napoleonic Wars from 1794 to 1801. He was impeached in 1806 for the mismanagement of navy funds but despite his acquittal he never returned to office. Pitt the Younger's death that same year may have contributed to his retiral from politics.

It has been claimed that the statue of Dundas in St Andrew's Square, Edinburgh intentionally faces away from the palace, in response to his having been offended by the king.

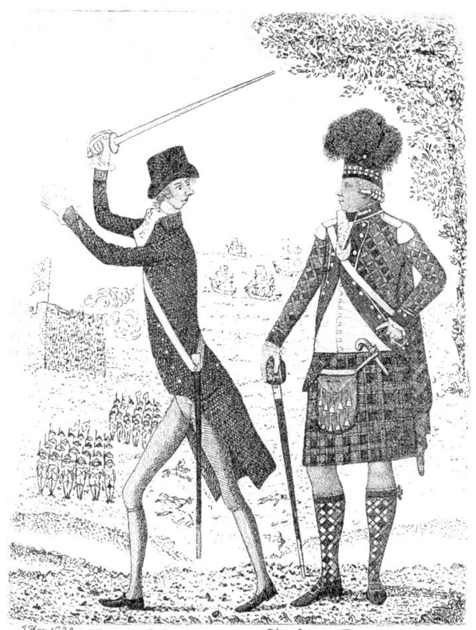

THE MODERN CAIN'S LAMENT

O Harrie whether shall I fly: I am this day. A Murderer
of thousands, Every one that finds me will count me his
Enemy and Slay me. ______

Alexander M'Kellar,
the Cock Of The Green (1803)

Golf is his religion

Alexander M'Kellar, though well known for his love of golf, never belonged to any club. He played on the Bruntsfield Links and was frequently found at the short holes by lamplight, having arrived there soon after breakfast. On one occasion, his wife, one of the earliest known golf widows, took his dinner and nightcap to him at the Links in the hope of embarrassing him. M'Kellar, totally unaware of the point being made, asked her to wait.

Although the Cock Of The Green did not play on the Sabbath, his love of the national sport did not abandon him, even in church. When Douglas Gourlay, a club and ball maker from Bruntsfield, for amusement, placed a golf ball on the collection plate, M'Kellar was quick to seize the prize ball for himself.

Kay was given the idea for the print by the same Douglas Gourlay and actually went to Bruntsfield to see M'Kellar in action and no doubt to check on the details of the club, which is presented as being very accurate for its time. On hearing of the incognito visit, M'Kellar exclaimed, 'What a pity! By gracious, if I had known I would have shown him some of my capers!'

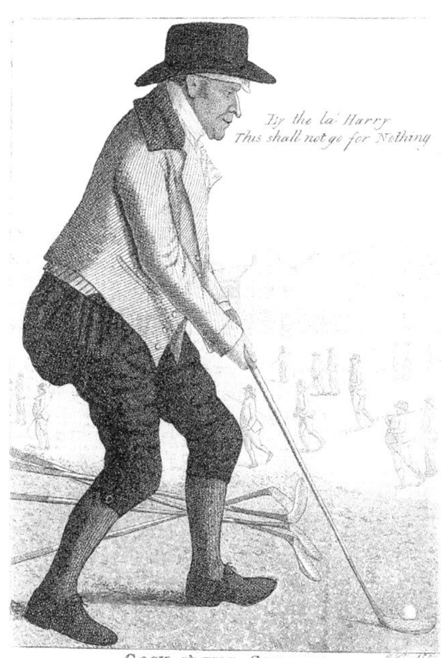

COCK OF THE GREEN.

Two Booksellers,
William Coke and John Guthrie (1810)

Cash on the nail

Though not close friends, Kay has chosen to put these two booksellers together because of their reputation for dealing in cash-only transactions. Hence the money pouch in Guthrie's hand.

William Coke was known as the father of the bookselling profession in Scotland. He was a bookseller in Leith and well known for his quick temper and quick deliveries. Feeling exhausted one day after completing an urgent delivery to the High Street he took refuge in the shop of his good friend, William Creech. There he sought to ease his aching head by applying whisky to his forehead. 'Bless me! What's that you are doing, Mr Coke?' asked Creech, to which Coke replied, 'Rubbing my head with whisky.' A bystander, Mr Miller, could not resist adding, 'No wonder that you are so very hot-headed!'

John Guthrie, known as 'ready-money John' started his bookselling business in the Canongate, later becoming a partner in Guthrie & Tait, booksellers in Nicolson Street. Not one to idle, while waiting on the next customer to come along, Guthrie would fill his time knitting stockings or working onion-nets to keep his hands busy and as he put it himself, to keep 'the devil out of his heart'.

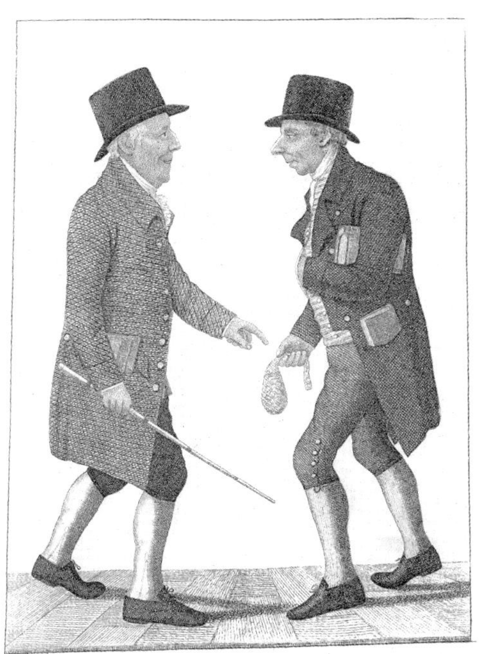
J KAY 1810

Connoisseurs: William Scott, James Sibbald, George Fairholme and James Kerr (1785)

Enthusing over prints

This is one of Kay's best known etchings, completed in 1785, and presents four amateur devotees of the fine arts with two anonymous figures in the background. David Allan's painting, 'The Connoisseurs' was done in 1783 and hangs in the National Gallery of Scotland.

William Scott, on the left, a plumber, is looking through his glass at a print of the 'Three Graces'. He was a known collector of engravings and had an extensive library.

James Sibbald, bookseller, is holding the print of the 'Three Graces' and appears to be looking intently at it. Sibbald bought the circulating library which had originally belonged to Allan Ramsay, and which latterly held 30,000 volumes. He also sold coloured engravings by foreign artists from his shop in Parliament Square but his business failed when customers discovered that it was actually Sibbald himself who was colouring the engravings.

George Fairholme, a shareholder in the Bank of Scotland, is holding a picture of William Martin, 'the grinning auctioneer'. The illiterate Martin once tried to read a French title in an auction, remarking, 'I am rather rusty in my French, but were it Hebrew, ye ken, I would be quite at hame!'

James Kerr, a music and fine arts enthusiast, set up the Leith Bank in 1801 but almost went bankrupt himself after losing at a card game with high stakes. When he recovered his losses it is said that he threw his cards on the table and vowed never again to take one in his hand.

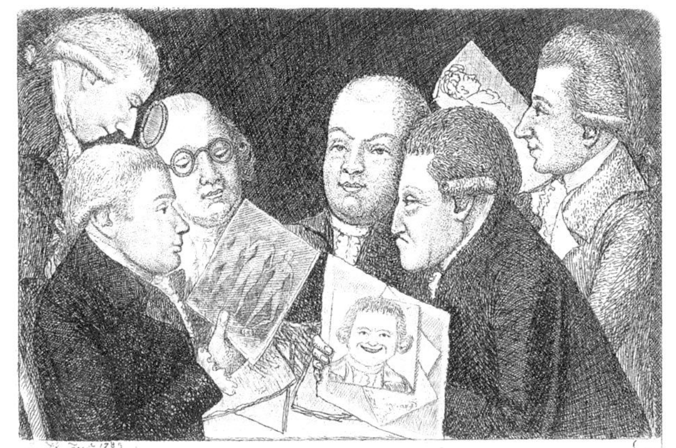

CONNOISSEURS

Courtship (1784)

Beauty is in the eye of the beholder

Kay's print would suggest that there is someone for everyone. Love, courtship, virtue and marriage were openly discussed in the enlightened society of eighteenth-century Scotland. Such issues featured prominently in Samuel Richardson's *Pamela*, an epistolary work, first published in 1740, and possibly the first fiction 'bestseller' of modern times, even spawning a new industry of souvenir cups and fans.

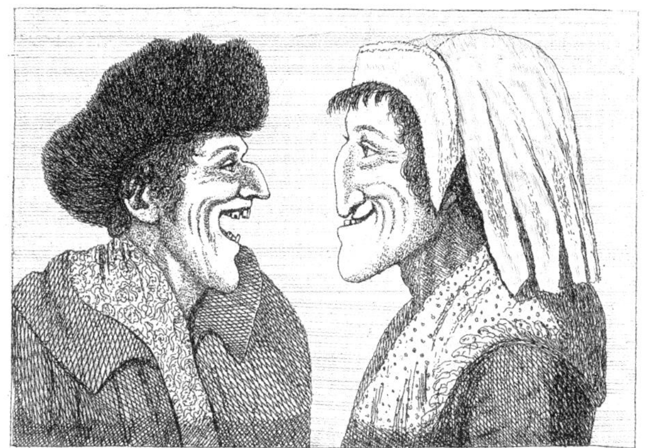

Courtſhip

Robert Craig of Riccarton, seated at the door of his own house in Princes Street (1815)

The joys of retirement and the open air

Robert Craig, a judge in the Commissary Court in Edinburgh, was the last male heir of Sir Thomas Craig of Riccarton, one of Scotland's greatest feudal lawyers. He lived at 91 Princes Street and Kay presents him here seated outside his front door with his faithful servant, William Scott. He never married and was known to many as a kindly man of liberal politics and with a fondness for fresh air and exercise, which no doubt contributed to his living to the grand old age of ninety-three years.

The Craig family took over the Riccarton estate, now the campus of Heriot-Watt University, in 1608 but with the death of Robert Craig in 1823 it passed to a distant relative, James Gibson Esq, a lawyer in Edinburgh. He was created a Baronet in 1831 and assumed the name of Gibson-Craig. The Riccarton estate was bought from the Gibson-Craig family by Midlothian Council in 1967 and formally gifted to Heriot-Watt University in 1969.

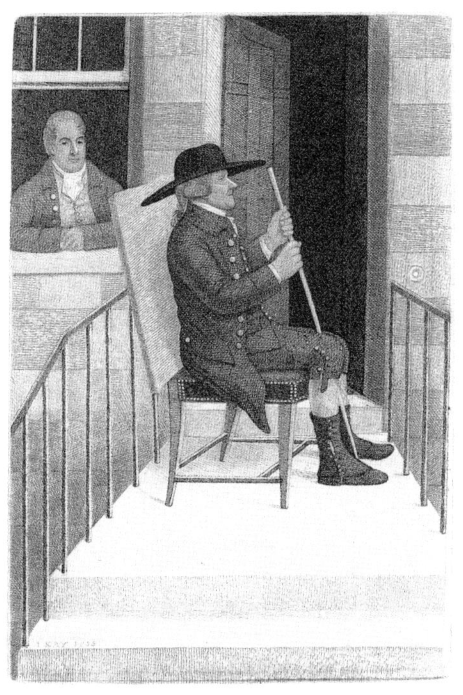

Dr Cullen in his study (1787)

Physician of the first water

William Cullen was a key figure in establishing Edinburgh as a world-class centre for medical teaching in the late eighteenth century. Born in Hamilton and educated in Glasgow, he was the first lecturer in chemistry at the University of Glasgow before moving on to become Professor of Chemistry and Medicine at Edinburgh and later President of the Royal College of Physicians of Edinburgh.

Cullen believed that normal health was maintained by 'nervous energy' and that disease was the result of disturbances in the nervous system. He condemned the use of laxatives and purgatives and prescribed only tonics such as quinine, camphor and, to the delight of many, wine in order to stimulate or sedate the nervous system. He coined the terms 'neurosis' and 'neuroses' a hundred years before psychiatrists and psychologists existed. Though an outstanding teacher of chemistry, Cullen published very little on the subject; indeed his children outnumbered his writings on chemistry by nine to one.

Cullen belonged to many clubs and was a great mimic. On one occasion in Nicholson's tavern at the foot of the West Bow he entertained the company by mimicking the probable remarks of the historian, Dr William Robertson, before his arrival. When Robertson came in and spoke the very same words, to howls of laughter, he realised what had happened and retorted, 'Gentlemen, I perceive somebody has been ploughing with my heifer before I came in.'

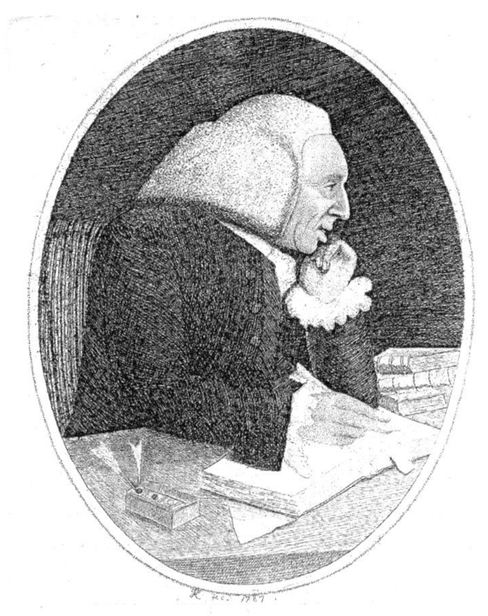

Robert Cullen, one of the
Senators of the College of Justice (1799)

A mimic at the bar

Robert Cullen was the eldest son of the celebrated Dr William Cullen (*XXIV*). He was made a Lord of Justiciary in 1799, which is the date of Kay's print and the date on the document in front of him.

As a youth, Cullen noticed that his father would listen to the request of his mother for money and hand over the required sum without ever looking up. Being a skilled mimic, like his father, when in need of some cash he would imitate his mother's voice and actions with great success. One day, however, the good doctor teased his wife with the words, 'What! Were you not here already?' His wife, agitated by the implication of his words, replied, 'No, indeed, I was not, my dear.' Young Cullen's scam was discovered and put paid to.

In later years Cullen mimicked his legal colleagues and he was often asked to show off his talent at legal dinners. On one occasion he went too far and mimicked the Lord President, who alone amongst the gathering, was not amused. Afterwards he warned the young jester, 'Very amusing, Mr Robert, very amusing, truly, ye're a clever lad – very clever; but just let me tell you, *that's no the way to rise at the bar!*'

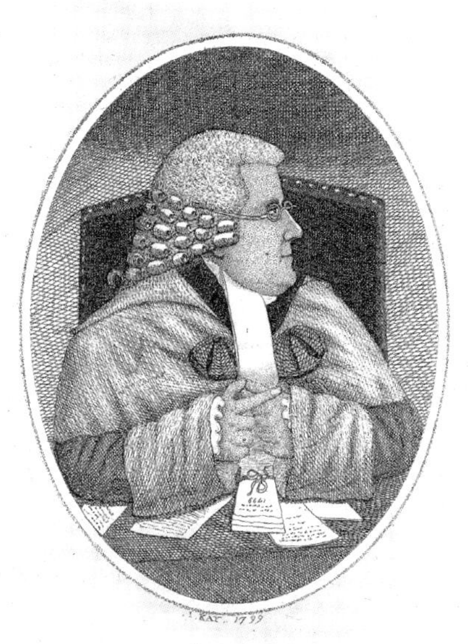

I. KAY. 1799.

Andrew Donaldson,
Teacher of Greek and Hebrew (1789)

A good scholar and sincere Christian

The eccentric teacher of Greek and Hebrew refused to adopt modern dress, preferring to go unshaven, without a wig, and covered up in an unfashionable greatcoat that reached his ankles. He never considered cleanliness to be next to godliness and remarked often that people gave themselves 'a great deal of unnecessary trouble' with domestic chores. He once said to a servant, 'Cannot you let the dust lie quietly. You stir it up only to get better mouthfuls of it.' Washing the floor brought further exasperation with the comment, 'Dear sirs, she'll wear all the boards rubbing them so.'

Andrew Donaldson was devoted to reading the Bible and Kay has presented him in his regular habit of reading the scriptures in the original Hebrew. He cared little for the profession of teaching and 'was sure Job never was a schoolmaster, otherwise we should not have heard so much about his patience'.

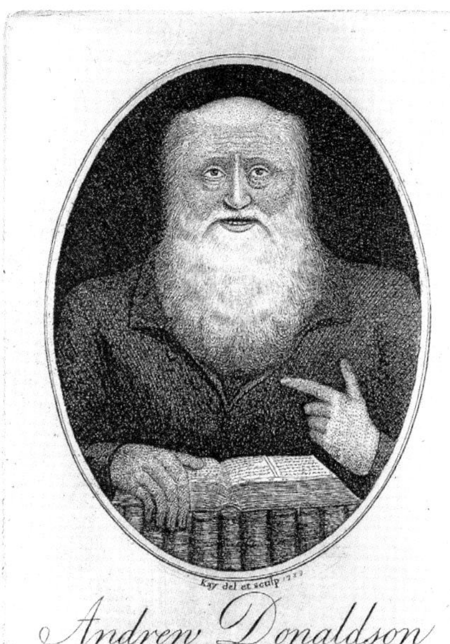

Andrew Donaldson

James Donaldson (1786)

A thirsty journeyman

James Donaldson was known as a half-witted journeyman baker of great strength. To amuse himself and others he would knock over a strong bull-calf with one blow of his fist. Kay alludes to the thirsty work in this print and by creating this likeness has deemed James Donaldson worthy of immortality.

O' Drouth

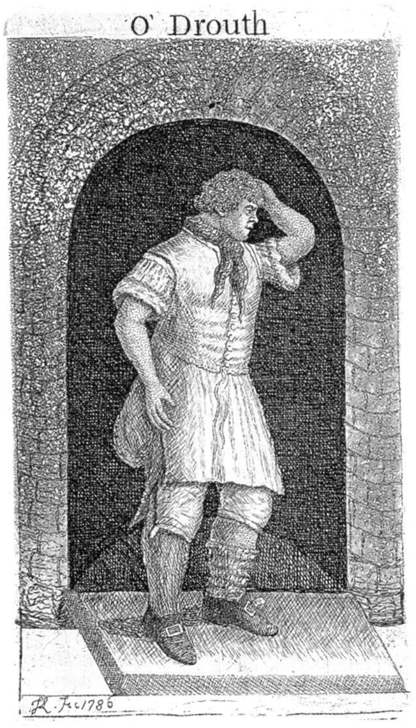

John Dowie, Vintner, Libberton's Wynd (1813)

An attentive innkeeper

Many of Edinburgh's greatest citizens crossed the well-worn threshold of John Dowie's tavern including Robert Fergusson, the poet, and David Hume. Dowie's was as famous for its food as its wine with clients offered minced collops or Nor'Loch eel-pie alongside wine, whisky or 'Edinburgh Ale' brewed by Archibald Younger at Croft-an-Righ near Holyrood.

John Dowie or 'dainty John' was known as the 'sleekest and kindest of landlords' and he would welcome guests with the words, 'Walk in, gentlemen, there's plenty o' corn in Egypt.'

Robert Burns frequented Dowie's during his time in Edinburgh and often sat in the smallest room in the tavern, known as 'The Coffin'. When John Dowie died in 1817 the new owner saw the potential of more business by renaming the tavern, *Burns Tavern*, late *Johnnie Dowie*.

John Dowie persisted in wearing an old-fashioned cocked hat until the end of his life but dispensed with his knee and shoe buckles and in this print, done just four years before his death in 1817, his shoes are clearly tied in the new fashion with laces.

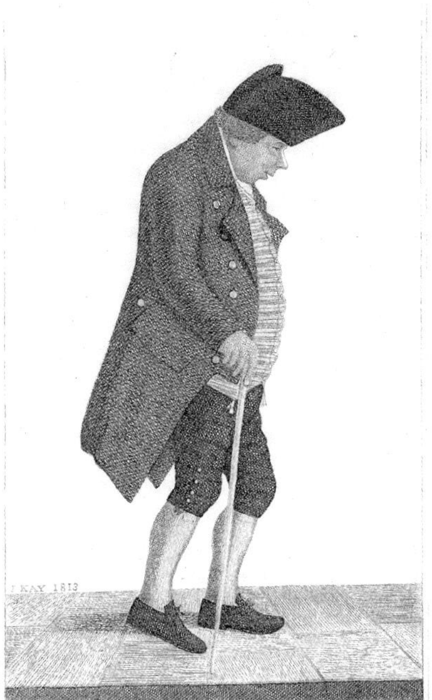

A' YE WHA WIS' ON E'ENINGS LANG, TO MEET AN' CRACK AN' SING A SANG
AN' WEET YOUR PIPES, FOR LITTLE WRANG, TO PURSE OR PERSON
TO SERE. JOHNNIE DOWIE'S GANG THERE THRUM A VERSE ON.

William Doyle, Samuel Sone, and William Foster (1784)

In hot pursuit of the fairer sex

Lieutenant William Doyle, the first figure on the left was a member of the 24th Regiment, which prior to coming to Edinburgh had seen service in Canada and in the American War of Independence. Mr Sone, surgeon, known as 'The Little Doctor' on account of his diminutive stature, was a close friend of Captain William Foster, also of the 24th Regiment, and Kay was no doubt taken with the contrast in height of the two men.

These two soldiers were known for their attentions to the fairer sex and so Kay has represented them escorting three celebrated belles of the day along the North Bridge.

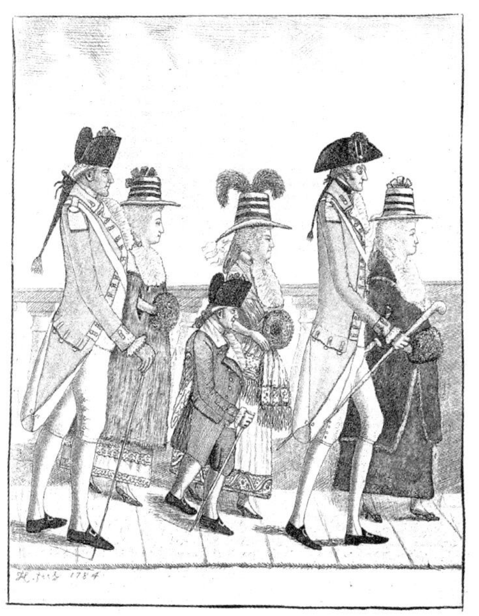

Dr Andrew Duncan, Senior,
Professor of the Theory of Medicine
in the University of Edinburgh (1797)

A true friend to the poor and needy

Dr Andrew Duncan was born in St Andrews but is best known for his contributions to medicine in Edinburgh. He founded the Royal Public Dispensary of Edinburgh in 1776 at West Richmond Street and provided free medical advice in an age when there was no outpatient care at the Royal Infirmary. Duncan presented individual cases to his medical students. This was the only public dispensary until 1815, when the Edinburgh New Town Dispensary was established. He was also President of the Royal College of Physicians and the first President of the Medico-Chirurgical Society in 1821.

Dr Duncan's name also lives on in the Andrew Duncan Clinic at the Royal Edinburgh Hospital, which was originally set up as a 'lunatic asylum' in 1807.

Outside medicine, Dr Duncan was an active member of numerous Edinburgh clubs including the Harveian and the Gymnastic Clubs. He was keen on keeping fit but perhaps it was vanity that sent him up Arthur's Seat every May Day for fifty years to wash his face in the morning dew, a custom said to ensure good looks as well as good health.

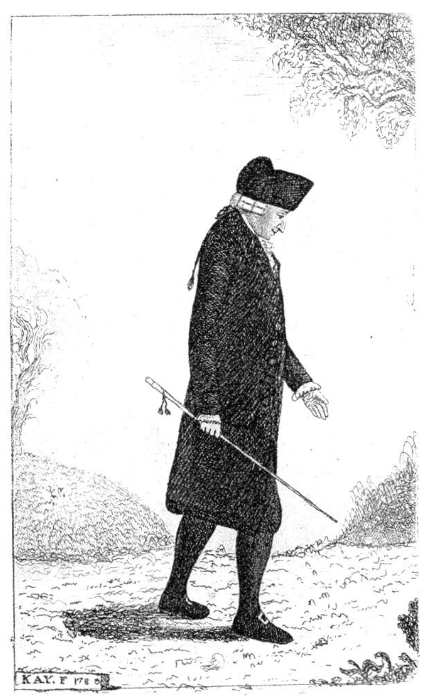
KAY. F 178 5

Henry Dundas and Sir James Stirling
'Patent for Knighthood' (1792)

Sir is well pleased

Henry Dundas, Home Secretary (later Lord Melville) (*see also XVIII*) was very unpopular on account of his use of patronage to secure political ends. He was MP for Edinburgh from 1790 to 1802 and was variously known as the 'uncrowned king of Scotland' and 'Harry the Ninth'.

In Kay's print of 1792 Sir James Stirling, Lord Provost of Edinburgh, is sheltering under Dundas's coat during the riots in Edinburgh that year when effigies of Dundas were burnt in public and the military had to be brought in to subdue political and social unrest. The Lord Provost got his knighthood later that year, hence the title of Kay's print.

On one occasion the Lord Provost was on a visit to the countryside and a passer-by pointed out Sir James attired in his velvet robes to a countrywoman. 'Is that the Lord Provost?' she exclaimed, 'I thocht it was the corpse rinnin' awa wi' the mort-cloth.'

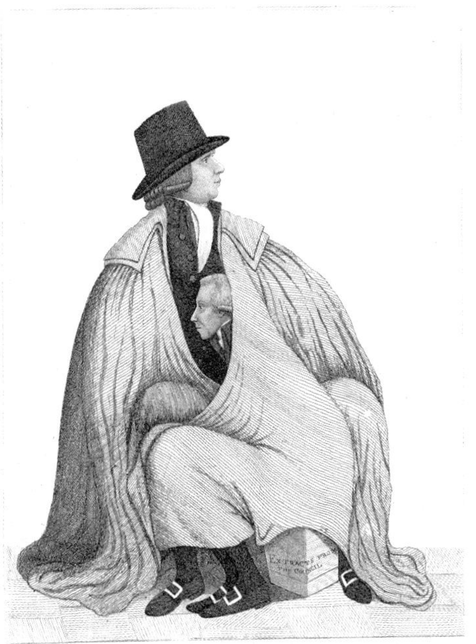

Patent for Knighthood.

The Earl of Errol and the Right Honourable Lord Haddo 'Two Noble Friends' (1787)

A youthful friendship

This is an early etching by Kay of two young noble friends in Edinburgh. To the left is George Hay, 16th Earl of Errol (1767–1798). His father, James Hay, was born with the name of James Boyd, son of Lord Kilmarnock, but legally changed it to James Hay in 1758, when he succeeded as Earl of Errol. George Hay succeeded his father in 1778, becoming 16th Earl of Errol and Lord High Constable of Scotland.

Lord Haddo, son of the 3rd Earl of Aberdeen, was Grand Master Mason of Scotland and laid the foundation stone of the South Bridge. He died prematurely after a fall from his horse.

His son, George Hamilton-Gordon, later 4th Earl of Aberdeen, served as Prime Minister from 1852 until 1855. It is said that he was one of Queen Victoria's favourite Prime Ministers and that it was he who persuaded the Queen to buy the Balmoral estate.

Haddo derives from the word 'Davoch', which was a unit of land that could be ploughed by an ox in a day. A 'half davoch' was half the size and this became abbreviated to Haddo.

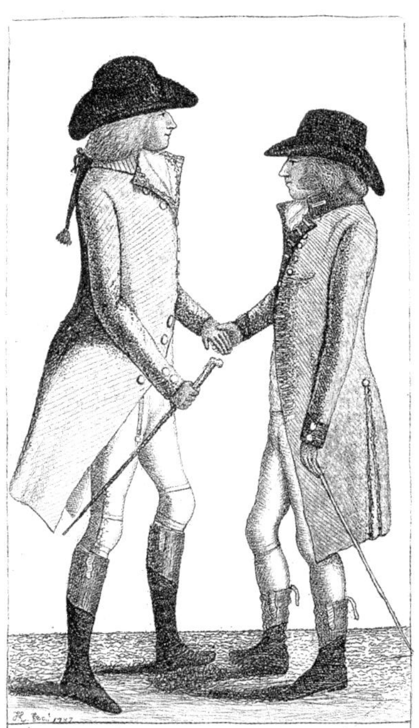

TWO NOBLE FRIENDS

The Honourable Henry Erskine,
Dean of the Faculty of Advocates (1790)

A prodigious punster

The Prince of Wales's coronet appears in the print because Erskine had just presided over a meeting of His Royal Highness's household in Edinburgh. The Latin motto, 'Seria mixta jocis' is an allusion to the humour and oratorical skills of Erskine at the bar.

Erskine was admitted to the Faculty of Advocates in 1765 and was the champion of rich and poor in the courts. One quote from a poor countryman illustrates his benevolence: 'There's no a puir man in a' Scotland need to want a friend or fear an enemy sae lang as Harry Erskine's to the fore.'

Famous for his ability to create puns, Erskine was willing to tease even those most eminent in their professions. It is told that on a walk with an English visitor along George Street in Edinburgh's New Town the visitor remarked how odd it was that St Andrew's Church should project so greatly while the Physicians Hall, immediately opposite, equally receded. Erksine agreed that George Street should have been 'the finest street in Europe' if only 'the forwardness of the clergy, and the backwardness of the physicians, had not marred its uniformity.' Physicians Hall has since 'receded' to Queen Street.

Henry Erskine died at his home at Almondell in West Lothian in 1817.

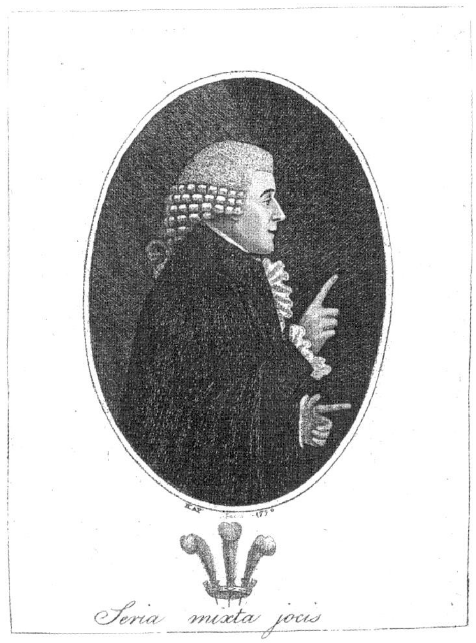

Seria mixta jocis

The Fiddler of Glenbirnie (1814)

Good for a reel or a rant

The musician's name is unknown but Glenbirnie or Glenburnie is a small hamlet near Newburgh in Fife. The Glenbirnie or Glenburnie Rant, a minor reel, is found in many collections including *The Gow Collection*, *The Athole Collection*, and Kerr's *Merry Melodies*.

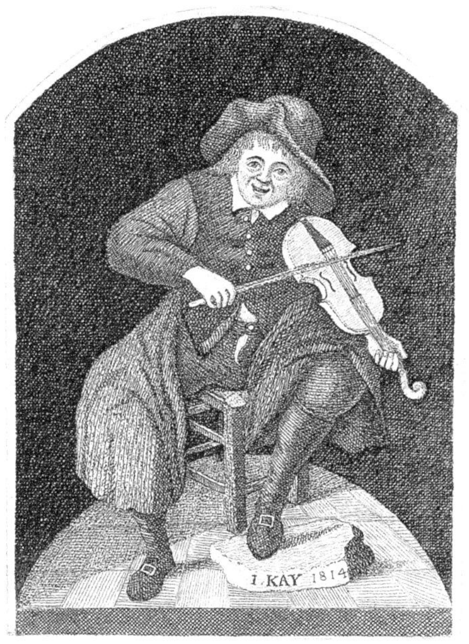

I. KAY 1814

The Edinburgh Fish-Women (1812)

'Wha'll o'caller ou!'

This print has embellished many a volume about Edinburgh and often without any acknowledgement to Kay.

The 'stout, clean and blooming' appearance of the fish-woman in Edinburgh was often commented on by locals and visitors alike. Her cry of 'Wha'll o' caller ou!' echoed up and down the High Street and at the corners of 'the draughty parallelograms' of the New Town.

Though nothing like the 'gin-swilling vixens of Billings-gate', many were dram-drinking fish-women and no wonder, given that they walked from Fisherrow or Newhaven carrying a basket weighing one hundred to two hundredweight of fish, ranging from haddocks and whitings to skate and lobsters.

One fish-woman heading home with her empty basket after a dram or two staggered into the path of the minister. 'What what Margaret!' the minister exclaimed. 'I think the road is rather narrow for you.' 'Hout sir,' replied Maggy, 'how can I gang steady without ballast?'

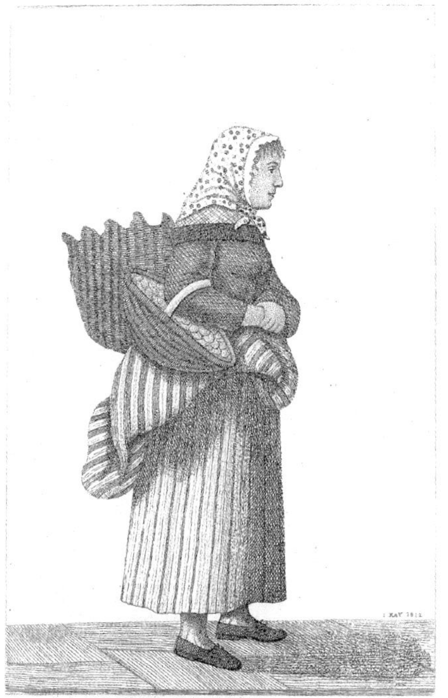

WHA'L O CALLER OYSTERS

Sir William Forbes of Pitsligo, Banker in Edinburgh (no date)

'The good shall mourn a brother, all a friend'

After completing his apprenticeship with the banking firm of John Coutts & Company, Sir William progressed to become head of the banking house of Sir William Forbes, Hunter & Co, Hunter being his great friend, Sir James Hunter Blair (*LIV*). The bank's prosperity was largely due to its having the remittance of the Excise duties from Edinburgh to London, which by 1780 involved some £350,000 per annum. Such a profitable account was quite a coup given that the three main joint stock banks at this time were the Bank of Scotland, the Royal Bank of Scotland and the British Linen Bank.

A modest man, Forbes attributed his business success to having a good partner, a choice he once confided to a friend as being, in importance, 'next to the choice of a wife'. He did not attend university but commented in an autobiographical essay that he 'did not dread any great disadvantage from that circumstance'.

Sir William was well known for his generosity and Kay shows a double view of him, first as the gentleman banker in his office, while through the window he is seen dispensing charity in Parliament Square. Although Sir William's son was to marry Williamina Belches Stuart, the first love of Sir Walter Scott, Scott knew the extent of Sir William's charity and wrote fondly of him:

Far may we search before we find
A heart so manly and so kind.

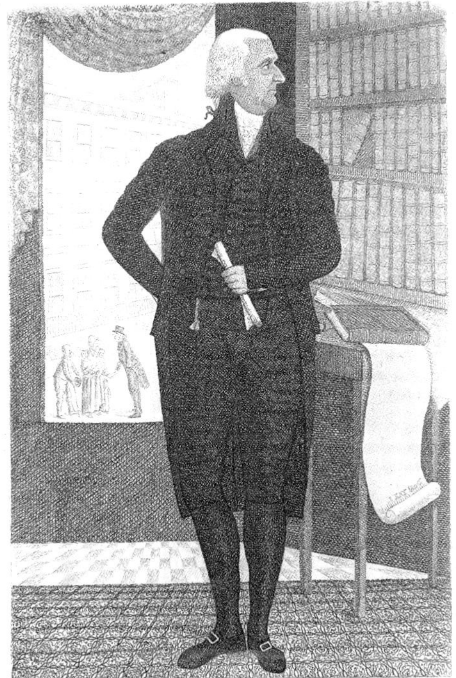

THE GOOD SHALL MOURN A BROTHER__ALL A FRIEND

Four Bucks: Dr Eiston, Signior Stabilini, Captain M'Kenzie and Macnab of Macnab 'Bucks have at you all or who's afraid.' (1786)

A motley quartet

First left is Dr Eiston, a well-known student dandy who later became an army surgeon. Across from him is Hieronymo Stabilini, a convivial Italian violinist who came to Edinburgh about 1778.

In the second row is Captain M'Kenzie, an army officer, who after an eventful career that included trial for murder, came back to Edinburgh in 1786. The Captain disliked being put alongside 'fiddlers and madmen' and even offered Kay a guinea to have it altered. Kay refused, but later supplied M'Kenzie with a miniature of himself for half a guinea.

Macnab of Macnab, the 'herculean Highlander', was known for the flashy gig that he used to attend the Leith races. At one event his horse died. When a 'waggish' race-goer at the next meeting enquired of Macnab, 'M'Nab, is that the same horse you had last year?' he got the quick reply, 'No, py Cot! But this is the same whip.' The race-goer fled. On another occasion, while in charge of the Breadalbane Fencibles, the Highlanders, with their propensity for smuggling, had packed a consignment of whisky, the 'peat reek', in the carts but unfortunately were stopped by the Excise men outside Alloa. When Macnab arrived, he accused the Excise men of being robbers, 'How dare you lay hands on his Majesty's stores?' The Excise men fled and Macnab told his men, 'Now, my lads proceed – your whisky's safe.'

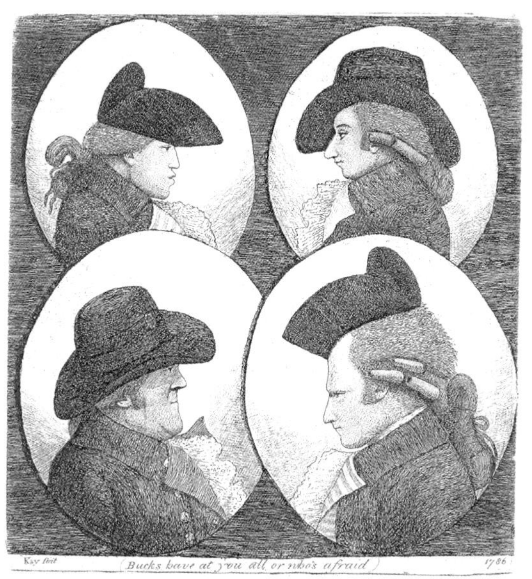

Kay fecit
(Bucks have at you all, or who's afraid)
1786

Thomas Fraser – (A Natural) (1784)

Anything for a dram

Thomas Fraser was fond of the 'dew' and would perform any song or dance in return for 'a dram and a sneeshin'. Kay presents him with glass in hand and about to salute the good lady who has supplied the contents of his glass. Fraser was a sweeper at the stables of Peter Ramsay, a vintner in the Cowgate, and the stables at Ramsay's inn also served as his 'kitchen, parlour and hall' as he had no home. He died in 1789.

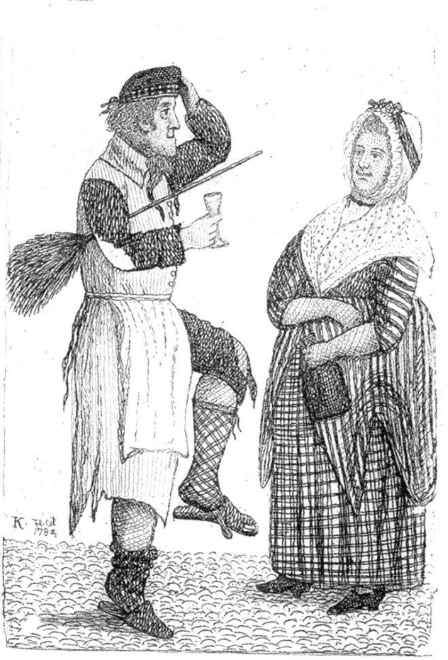

Francis Anderson, WS, James Hunter, and his son, George Hunter
'The Friendly Invitation' (1802)

Can you hear me?

Kay probably witnessed this scene from his shop window in Parliament Square.

James Hunter, a wealthy merchant, is inviting Francis Anderson, a Writer to the Signet who had offices in Royal Exchange Square, to dinner. Hunter is leaning over to accommodate the excessive deafness of his friend.

Thought of as a confirmed bachelor, Francis Anderson married a Miss Martin who some felt was not an appropriate choice. When asked by the Earl of Wemyss one day how he came to 'marry his sister's waiting-maid', Anderson replied, 'I couldna be fashed courting a lady; for weel did I ken nae lady would tak' a lang-leggit, deaf, thick shankit – like me; besides, I liked the lassie, and the lassie liked me; an' that's the way I took her.' It was a happy marriage and produced five children!

George Hunter on the left resented being made to look shorter than his father in the print.

Known as 'English George' due to his affected accent, he had a business on the South Bridge selling supplies and uniforms to the volunteer and militia corps. On hearing of George IV's visit in 1822 he recognised the business opportunity and postponed his planned retirement. Hunter supplied the Highland dress worn by His Majesty (at a cost of £1,354) as well as national uniforms to a great many of the nobility who attended the royal occasion. In three weeks he amassed a handsome fortune of £30,000.

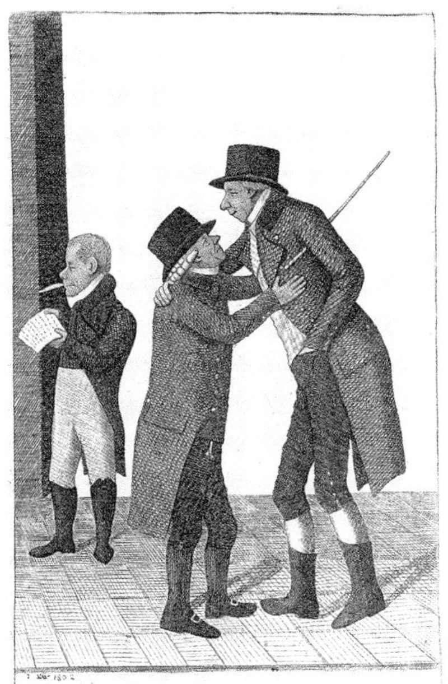

THE FRIENDLY INVITATION

James Gillespie of Spylaw and his brother John Gillespie (1797)

Philanthropist and snuff merchant

James, who appears to the left of the print, was the elder of the two brothers and the establishment of James Gillespie's Hospital and School in Edinburgh was the result of an endowment from him in 1803.

John Gillespie looked after the snuff shop in the High Street while James, known as 'the laird' remained at Spylaw House in Colinton and took charge of the snuff-grinding mill.

He kept a carriage for which the Hon. Henry Erskine (*XXXIII*) gave a motto:

> Wha wad hae thocht it,
> That noses had bocht it.

The same motto could also be applied to James Gillespie's School.

Gillespie's snuff shop was at 231 High Street in the Old Town. At the time of making this print Kay was living in a flat above the shop and it is said he received five pounds to suppress the print. More likely this was the fee paid for the handsome miniature.

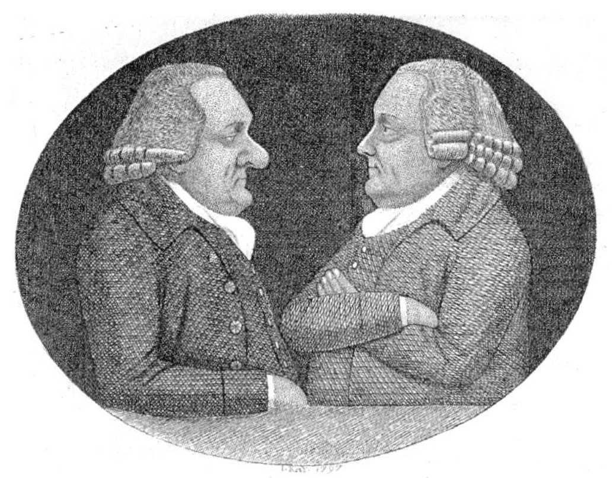

Dr Glen and the
Daft Highland Laird (1784)

Objects of ridicule

Dr Glen was well known for his frugal gestures. Despite his great wealth he once enquired as to the possibility of having a second-hand coffin for his wife, and no doubt a body snatcher might well have obliged him.

The Daft Laird was James Robertson of Kincraigie, an ardent Jacobite who having survived the '45 only wanted to be hanged, drawn and quartered for the Stuart cause. All his rants against the House of Hanover and public toasts to the 'king over the water' were to no avail so he took to carving likenesses of those he disliked on a walking stick and held it up for all to see. The carvings changed daily and in this print Kay shows the heads of Dr James Graham (*XLVI*), the quack doctor, on top and Principal William Robertson underneath. However on one occasion Kay himself became the subject and when a passer-by enquired of the Daft Laird as to the identity of his new victim he quickly replied, 'Don't you see it's the barber?'

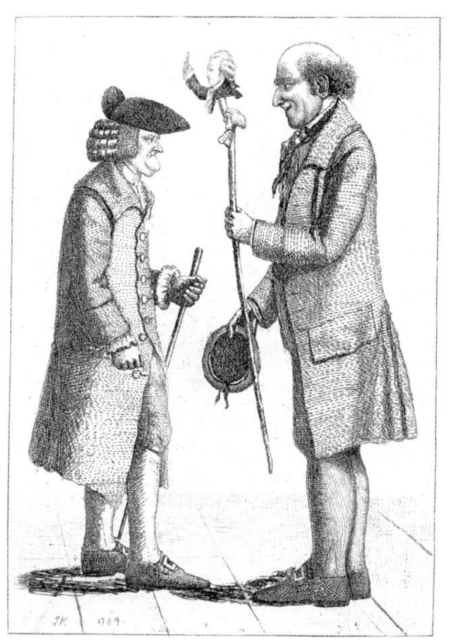

Right Hon. Lord Adam Gordon and HRH the Count d'Artois, afterwards Charles X (1796)

The rough with the smooth

Kay created this print in 1796, soon after the arrival at Holyrood of the Count d'Artois, brother of the executed Louis XVI. The royal arrival was a major event in the city and the beginning of a long period of exile in Scotland for the future Charles X of France.

The Count was considered the most handsome member of the French royal family and according to the Comte d'Hezecques, 'few beauties were cruel to him'. He came to Holyrood as a refugee from massive debts incurred elsewhere and was described by one observer as 'the most gay, gaudy, fluttering, accomplished, luxurious and expensive Prince in Europe'. Despite this, major refurbishments to the tune of £2,600 were carried out at Holyrood Palace in advance of his arrival, which included fitting new carpets, creating a private chapel in the Great Gallery and installing a billiard room in the former Guard Chamber.

As Charles X, the last Bourbon king, on hearing of the great fire in Edinburgh's Old Town in 1824, he sent a generous donation for the relief of those who suffered as a result.

The count is seen here with Lord Adam Gordon, soldier and Member of Parliament, who had been appointed Commander in Chief in Scotland in 1789 and Governor of Edinburgh Castle in 1796.

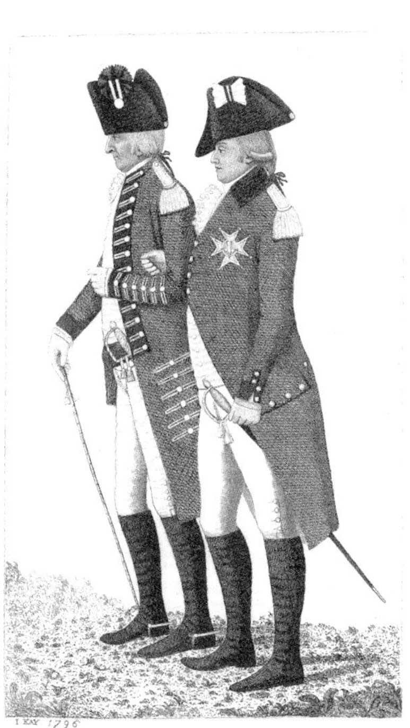

Captain George Gordon, Captain George Robertson and John Grieve, Lord Provost of Edinburgh (no date)

A civic trio

Captain Gordon, the leftmost figure, is seen in attendance on the central figure of Lord Provost Grieve. Little is known of the Captain but that he had seen service in Holland as an officer of the Scottish Brigade and was known in Edinburgh for partaking frequently of a morning tipple. Captain Robertson, to the right, appears to be receiving instructions from Provost Grieve as Captain of the Town Guard. When Captain Robertson died in 1787 Captain Gordon took over his role as Captain of the Town Guard.

John Grieve, a merchant in the Royal Exchange was twice Lord Provost of Edinburgh, from 1782–3 and again 1786–7. In 1788 he was appointed one of his Majesty's Commissioners of Excise.

Grieve was instrumental in the raising of The Mound or Mud Brig, the causeway created with two million cartloads of earth and rubbish from the building of the New Town. It was claimed that the east side of the Mud Brig was started a little eastward of the line of Hanover Street, opposite Grieve's door, as an arrangement 'particularly intended for the convenience' of the Lord Provost.

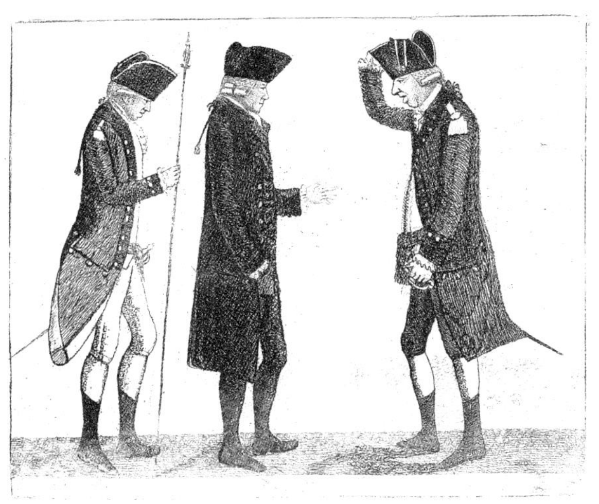

Sergeant-Major Patrick Gould of the 1st Regiment of Edinburgh Volunteers (1797)

Drillmaster of the 'Bellygerents'

Sergeant-Major Patrick Gould was responsible for training recruits to the new Royal Edinburgh Volunteers, many of whom belonged to the professional classes, such as William Creech, the publisher and Henry Dundas, later Viscount Melville (*XVIII, XXXI*), who chose to assume the humble rank of private.

The drill sergeant was a tough task master and the portly volunteer portrayed in Kay's print, James Laing, a saddler in South Bridge Street, is a reference to Gould's nickname for his recruits – the 'Bellygerents' on account of their 'ample' physique. When asked by a friend, 'Pray, who is that you are drilling in the Print done by Kay?' Gould answered in his typical brusque fashion, 'I can't say, sir, unless you turn him to the right-about-face.'

Gould's attitude to military discipline is best put in his own words: 'Steady, gentlemen, steady; a soldier is a mere machine. He must not move – he must not speak – and as for thinking, no! no! – no man under the rank of a field-officer is allowed to think!' No doubt this was a challenge for many of his 'professional' recruits.

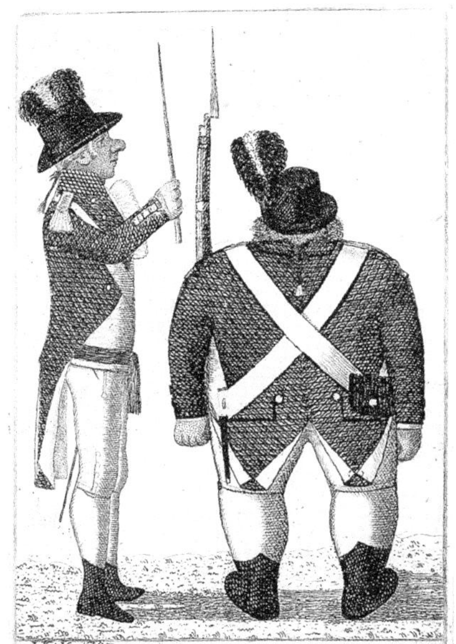

TO THE RIGHT ABOUT——FACE

The Most Noble Marquis of Graham and the Right Hon. the Earl of Buchan (1784)

A Caledonian duet

This early print of 1784 by Kay presents the subjects in the 'garb of old Gaul' beating up for a volunteer body called the Caledonian Band. Like its prototype, the Edinburgh Defensive Band, it later converted into a body of Freemasons, of which the Earl of Buchan was made Master.

The Marquis, later the 3rd Duke of Montrose, to the left of the print, is given the credit for removing the 1782 law prohibiting Highlanders from wearing the kilt. He held many honours and distinctions, being a Knight of the Thistle and of the Garter, and for many years Chancellor of the University of Glasgow.

David Stewart Erskine, 11th Earl of Buchan, devoted most of his life to literary and antiquarian pursuits. In 1780 he founded the Society of Antiquaries of Scotland, the second oldest antiquarian society in Britain, which was incorporated by Royal Charter in 1783. He acquired the lands of Dryburgh Abbey in 1786 and had plans to create a Temple of Caledonian Fame in the chapter-house. This may well have prompted Sir Walter Scott's description of him as 'a person whose immense vanity, bordering upon insanity, obscured or rather eclipsed very considerable talents'.

Erskine is also known to have helped the enigmatic army surgeon James Miranda Barry, claimed to be the world's first female doctor, while a medical student at the University of Edinburgh from 1809 to 1812.

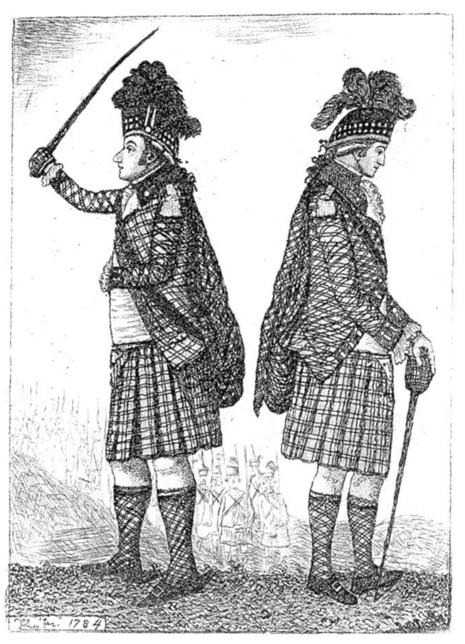

Dr James Graham going along the North Bridge in a high wind (1785)

Fanatic, fraud or clever marketeer?

Kay portrays the eccentric Dr Graham pursuing a Miss Dunbar along the North Bridge, no doubt in reference to his penchant for the ladies and his exploits as a sexologist.

Graham studied medicine in Edinburgh but never graduated. He is best known for his Temple of Health and Hymen in Pall Mall in London, where he installed his famous celestial bed. For £50 a night childless and impotent couples could sleep on this bed, which had fifteen hundredweight of magnets and electrical machines built into it and which could move on an axis and tilt at the vital moment to assist in conception. Success rates are not known for many clients wished to remain anonymous. One of Graham's assistants is claimed to be Amy or Emma Lyon, better known for her later role as Emma Hamilton, mistress of Lord Nelson.

A staunch vegetarian, Graham refused to wear wool but slept on a hair mattress, and was so convinced of the benefits of fresh air that he once considered building a house on Arthur's Seat. On the other hand he was said to inhale an ounce or two of ether each day 'with manifest placidity and enjoyment'.

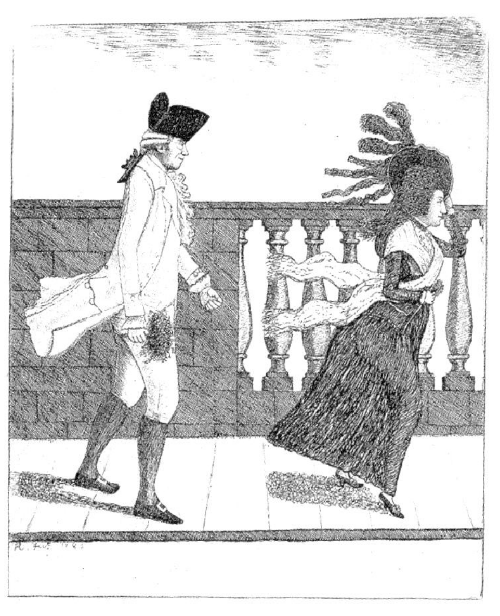

Dr Gregory Grant, Physician (1799)

Medic and musical host

Dr Gregory Grant was a much sought-after physician in Edinburgh, not just for his skills as a physician but also for the many 'musical suppers' held at his home in James's Court, just off the Royal Mile. Guests included Sir John Sinclair, the Duchess of Gordon and the actress, Sarah Siddons.

Though less fanatical than his brother Colquhoun Grant (*LXV*) about the Stuart cause, Dr Grant was nevertheless a great admirer of Highland culture. He believed there was no raiment in Europe to compare with Highland dress when worn by a native Highlander and that no language could convey meaning with more clarity than the Gaelic. He actively supported the Highland Society of Edinburgh set up in 1784, now known as The Royal Highland and Agricultural Society of Scotland. He was the first to suggest that prizes be offered for the improvement of the Highlands, which led to medals being offered for essays on the management of cattle and the cultivation of grasses and green crops.

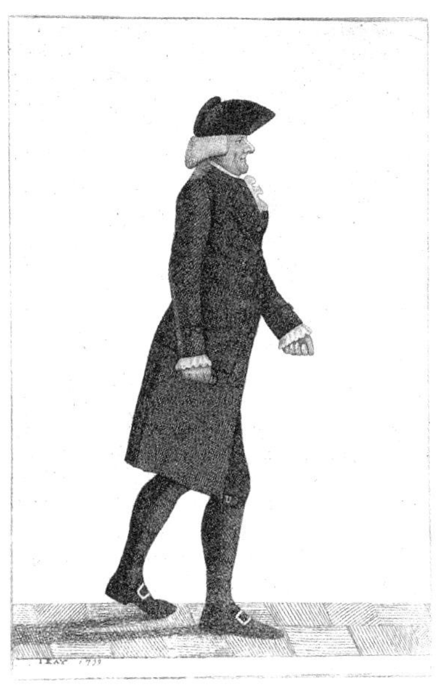

Dr James Gregory, Professor of the Practice of Medicine in the University of Edinburgh (1797)

Creator of Gregory's Powder or Mixture

James Gregory was the creator of Gregory's Powder, a mixture of pulverised rhubarb, ginger and magnesia, prescribed as a laxative. In 1778 James became Professor of the Institutes of Medicine at Edinburgh and in 1790 succeeded William Cullen (*XXIV*) as Professor of the Practice of Physic.

Though a competent scholar, teacher and physician, Gregory had a reputation for being argumentative. He was implicated in a defamation case with a Dr Hamilton whom he beat with a stick, and was fined £100 for the deed.

For all that, he was one of the first recruits to the newly formed Royal Edinburgh Volunteers in 1793 but still managed to irritate his drillmaster. Sergeant Gould (*XLIV*) said of him, 'He might be a good physician, but he was a very awkward soldier.' He tormented Gould continuously with questions and after one question too many, Gould shouted at the good doctor, 'D**n it, sir, you are here to obey orders, and not to ask reasons; there is nothing in the King's orders about reasons!' Gregory persuaded Gould to give him some personal instruction but it was to no avail, with Gould lamenting, 'Hold your tongue, sir; I would rather drill ten clowns than one philosopher!'

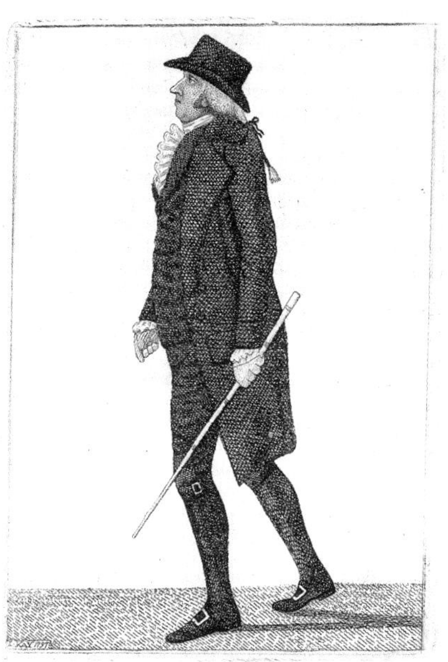

Captain Francis Grose, FAS
of London and Perth (1789)

Antiquarian and bon viveur

Robert Burns met Captain Grose in 1789 when he was in Scotland collecting material for his *Antiquities of Scotland*. Burns described him as a 'cheerful-looking grig of an old fat fellow' and declared that he had never met anyone of 'more original observation, anecdote and remark'. For the second volume of his *Antiquities of Scotland*, Grose accepted Burns' recommendation to include a drawing of Alloway Kirk but on condition that his 'worthy friend Mr Burns' would provide a witch's tale to go with it. We are indebted to Grose for this witch's tale, better known as 'Tam O'Shanter'.

As well as his *Antiquities of Scotland* and the earlier *Antiquities of England and Wales*, Grose also compiled a pioneering work on slang, *The Classical Dictionary of the Vulgar Tongue*, published in 1785. This fascinating collection of words and phrases from the eighteenth century includes entries such as 'ANDREA FERRARA', a famous sword-cutler whose name marked most Highland broadswords or claymores and later became the common name for them, a 'RUM DUKE' meaning a queer, unaccountable fellow and 'FLAYBOTTOMIST' referring to a schoolteacher.

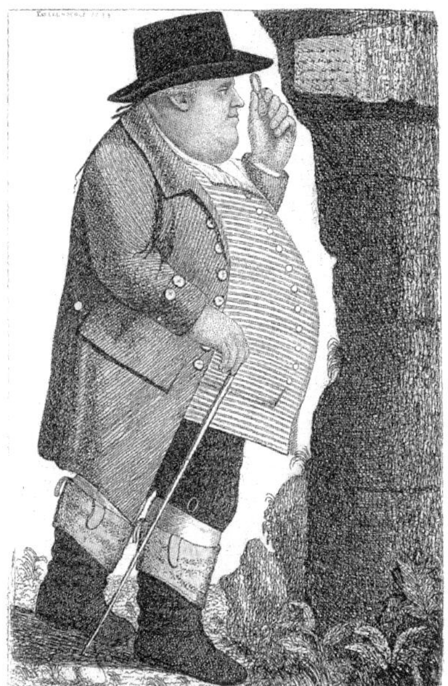

THE *British Antiquarian*

Dr Alexander Hamilton, Professor of Midwifery (1786)

One of the last to maintain a personal sedan chair

The two ladies in the background are anonymous, but are probably placed here as an allusion to the specialist skills of Dr Hamilton.

When Kay produced this print in 1786, Alexander Hamilton had been sole Professor of Midwifery at the University of Edinburgh for three years. He became Deacon of the Incorporation of Surgeons and Barbers in 1776 and during his tenure the Incorporation received its Royal Charter from George III on 14 March 1778. Henceforth the Incorporation was titled the Royal College of Surgeons of the City of Edinburgh with the title of Deacon being changed to President and all members subsequently being called Fellows.

Dr Hamilton was one of the first to provide proper classes for training midwives and he partly funded the new lying-in hospital in Edinburgh in the early 1790s. His numerous writings on midwifery became standard texts for teaching and were translated into German.

His son took over the Chair of Midwifery in 1800 but Dr Hamilton held on to his personal sedan chair, which was one of about fifty private chairs in Edinburgh at a time when the horse-drawn carriage was starting to make inroads as a new city centre transport system.

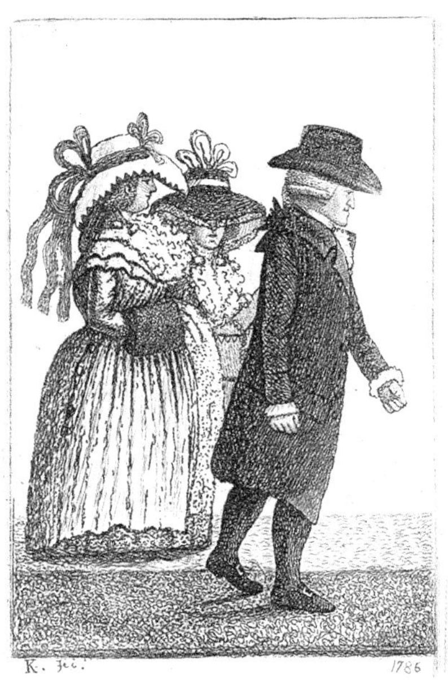

K. fec.
1786

Dr James Hamilton, Senior (1789)

Cocked-hat Hamilton

Dr Hamilton was old-fashioned in dress and manner and was said to be the last person to wear the three-cornered hat, so earning him the nickname, 'Cocked-hat Hamilton'. He gave his cast-off hats to Ebenezer Wilson (*XCIX*), ringer of the Tron Kirk bell. He was one of Edinburgh's best known physicians, at various times being Physician to the Royal Infirmary, George Heriot's, the Merchant Maiden and the Trades' Maiden Hospitals. Dr Hamilton died in 1835 at his home in St Andrew Square, next door to his namesake, Dr James Hamilton, Junior.

He was for many years an active member of many clubs and was a close friend of Dr Andrew Duncan, Senior (*XXX*) and the surgeon known as Lang Sandy Wood (*C*). The following lines were written to describe the three of them:

'Twas Andrew the merry and Jamie the good,
In a hackney coach had ta'en home Sandy Wood.

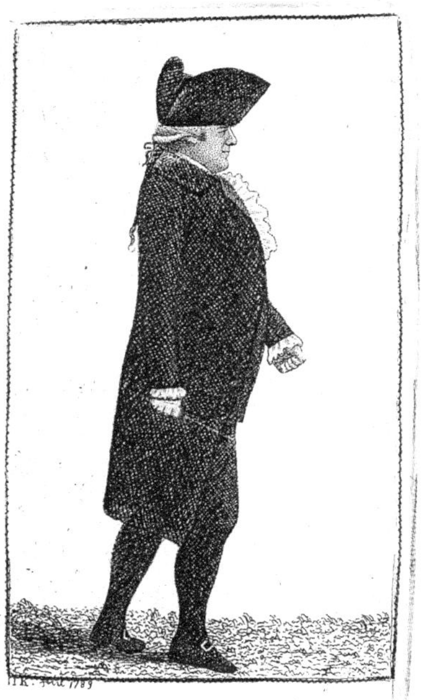

Sir Archibald Hope of Pinkie
'Knight of the Turf' (1789)

A wealthy horseman

Sir Archibald Hope succeeded to the title on the death of his grandfather, Sir Thomas Hope, the man who laid out Hope Park in Edinburgh, better known today as the Meadows.

With no desire to enter the professions or politics, Sir Archibald established extensive salt and coal works on his estate and in due course amassed great wealth. He was known for his collection of 'neighing steeds' and 'deep-mouthed hounds' and in 1789 was elected President of the Caledonian Hunt. This is the date of Kay's print and the artist makes a reference to his new position in its title, 'Knight of the Turf'.

Sir Archibald entertained extensively at his home, but the most famous visitors to Pinkie had come in earlier times, namely Charles I as a young prince and Bonnie Prince Charlie who stayed here after the Battle of Prestonpans. Pinkie House is now part of Loretto School in Musselburgh.

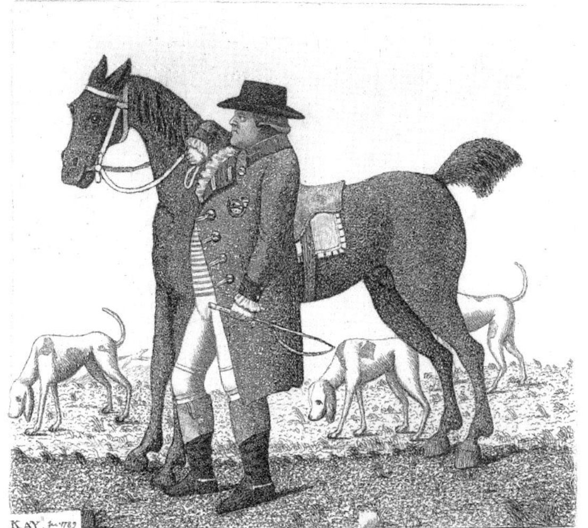

KNIGHT of the ·TURF

Professor John Hope, Professor of Botany in the University of Edinburgh (1786)

Unsung hero of the Royal Botanic Garden

This is the only known likeness of Professor John Hope, one of Scotland's most accomplished medics and botanists. It was Hope who introduced the Linnaean system for cataloguing plants into Scotland and he who secured permanent Crown funding for the first Royal Botanic Garden in Edinburgh, with himself as Regius Keeper. No doubt some readers of these pages will also appreciate his having planted the first rhubarb seeds in Edinburgh.

In 1763 Hope supervised the removal of the plant collections from the Physic Gardens at Holyrood and east of the Trinity Hospital (near the present-day Waverley) to a new 'out-of-town' site on Leith Walk. Kay's print shows Hope with an unidentified gardener in the new Botanical garden, an area of around five acres between present-day Annandale Street and McDonald Road.

He commissioned Robert Adam in 1779 to design a monument to Linnaeus which was later executed by James Craig. Hope paid for the monument himself and it now stands north of the glasshouses at the Royal Botanic Garden in Edinburgh, which was established finally at Inverleith in 1823.

Hope's name lives on in the *genus Hopea*, a genus of trees from south-east Asia, and in the street named Hope Crescent, now known as Hopetoun Crescent. Like John Kay, Professor Hope had no gravestone for over two hundred years. Now their respective twenty-first-century memorials are almost side by side at the north-west corner of Greyfriars Kirkyard, by the Flodden Wall.

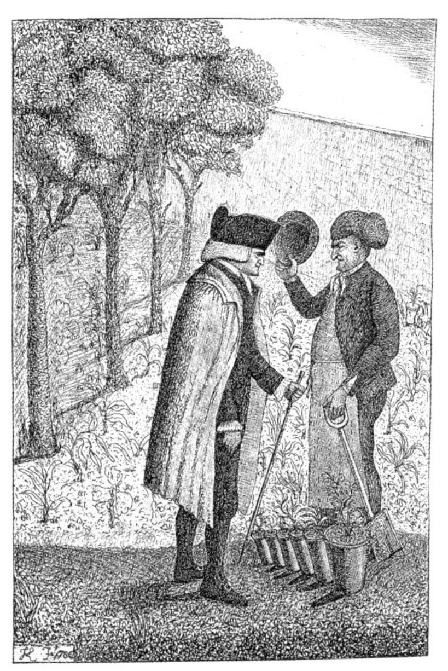

Sir James Hunter Blair, Bart,
late Lord Provost of Edinburgh (1785)

Banker and promoter of municipal improvements

Sir James Hunter Blair was a successful banker in Edinburgh and a partner in Sir William Forbes, James Hunter & Co, one of the few banks to survive the 'Black Wednesday' crash of 10 June 1772. He later entered politics as MP for Edinburgh before becoming Lord Provost in 1784 and in 1786 he was given a knighthood. Hunter Square and Blair Street in Edinburgh are named after him.

Kay presents Hunter Blair in his robes of office as Lord Provost of Edinburgh, with a copy of a plan of the South Bridge in his right hand. This print was a commission for which Kay received a guinea for the first impression and then half-a-guinea for a further dozen. Hunter Blair masterminded the controversial plan for the South Bridge and was also involved in the contentious plans for levelling the High Street, the subject for another of Kay's satirical prints (*LXII*).

James Hunter took the name of Blair when his wife Jean Blair inherited her father's estate at Dunskey, near Portpatrick, in 1777. They had fourteen children, eight of whom are depicted with their parents at Dunskey House, in a painting by the Scottish artist David Allan which now hangs at Blairquhan. Blairquhan was bought from the Whitefoord family by Sir James's son David. While good fortune shone on Sir James on Black Wednesday, the Whitefoords suffered severe losses with the collapse of the Ayr bank.

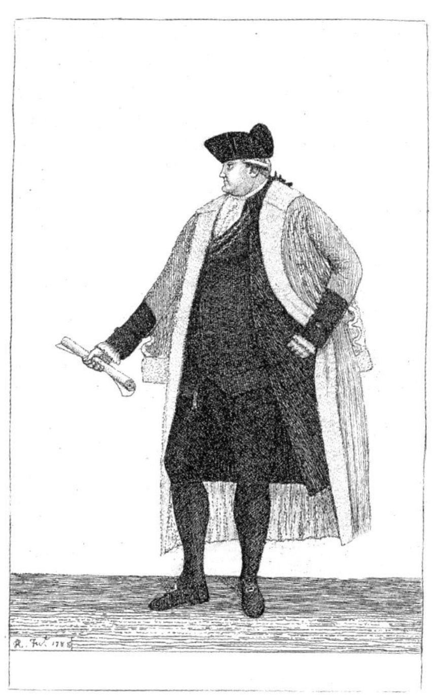

Dr James Hutton (1787)

Father of modern geology

Along with close friends such as Adam Smith (*LXXXVII*) and Joseph Black (*VIII*), James Hutton was one of the intellectual giants of the Scottish Enlightenment. It is interesting to note that Kay's print of 1787 shows Hutton studying rock formations that have face profiles outlined in the rock, perhaps a reference to the critics of his theories.

A medical graduate of Leyden in 1749, Hutton spent some years farming before moving back to Edinburgh around 1768. His *Theory of the Earth* was first read at the meeting of the Royal Society of Edinburgh in 1785 but was not published until 1788. Hutton proposed a universe very different to the Biblical one. He suggested that natural forces had shaped the Earth's surface, not over a period of 6,000 but over millions of years, and there was 'no vestige of a beginning, no prospect of an end'. It was a revolutionary theory and took many years to find general acceptance in the face of opposition from the Creationists.

Hutton's home at St John's Hill in Edinburgh, once described as 'so full of fossils and chemical apparatus that there is hardly room to sit down,' has been demolished and is now the location of the James Hutton Memorial Garden.

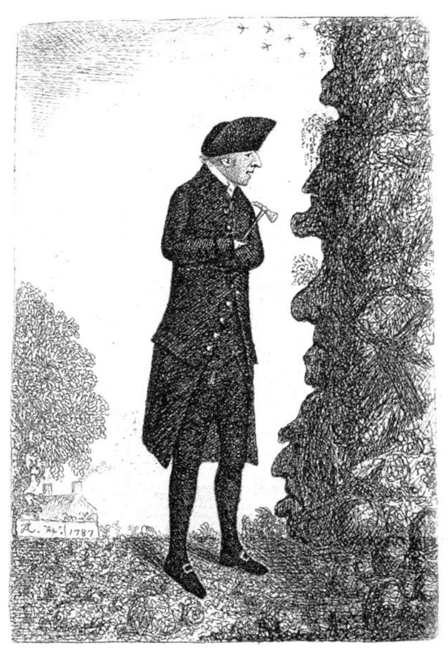

Francis Jeffrey, Advocate, one of the Senators of the College of Justice (1816)

The Whig amongst the Tories

Francis Jeffrey, judge and literary critic, was co-founder and editor of *The Edinburgh Review*, founded in 1802. Regarded as an organ of Whig propaganda by some, *The Review* was unique in having editorial independence and in time it became the most influential journal of literary criticism in Britain.

Jeffrey's criticism often offended and his duel with Thomas Moore in 1806 had to be stopped by police. Lord Byron decided the pen was mightier and penned his *English Bards and Scottish Reviewers* as a retaliatory piece in 1809, unaware that it was in fact Henry Brougham who had ridiculed his *Hours of Idleness* in *The Review.*

Jeffrey's Whig leanings may have prejudiced his legal prospects which did not improve until 1816, the year when separate juries were established in the Court of Session. Kay's etching of 1816 may well be illustrating Jeffrey's intellectual prowess and eloquence in a closing appeal to a jury in a civil case.

Jeffrey resigned from *The Review* to enter politics in 1830 and was responsible for the Scottish Reform Bill of 1831, which allowed the citizens of Edinburgh to vote him in as a Member of Parliament in 1833. He gave up politics on his appointment as a Judge of the Court of Session.

The Edinburgh Review relocated to London in 1847 but is now based back in Edinburgh.

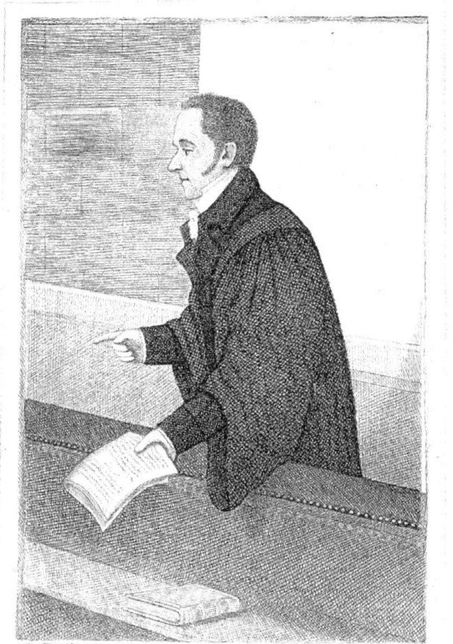
I KAY 1816

Robert Johnston and Sibilla Hutton (1786)

Rotund Retailers

Kay no doubt knew both of these corpulent shopkeepers who had premises in the Royal Exchange but there is no evidence of them having been friends.

Robert Johnston was a partner in the banking firm of Johnston and Smith at the Royal Exchange. Along with other misfortunes, the loss of over £800 in a robbery in 1768, probably carried out by the infamous Deacon Brodie (*LXXXVIII*), led to the closure of the bank. Johnston then became a grocer.

Sibilla Hutton, a daughter of the manse, was an eighteenth-century fashion addict, and few could match the swiftness with which she flaunted *la mode du jour*. Her father despaired of her extravagant dress and even harsh words from the pulpit did not convince her of the need to dress more plainly. When the minister warned her, 'Sibby! Sibby! Do you really expect to get to heaven with such a bonnet on your head?' Sibilla was most defensive in her reply, 'And why not father? I'm sure I'll make a better appearance than you will do in that vile, old-fashioned black wig, which you have worn for these last twenty years!' Neither did a later sermon on female vanity, which referred specifically to Sibilla's outrageous bonnet, have any effect. Only when fashion dictated a different style did Sibilla chose to abandon the flamboyant headdress.

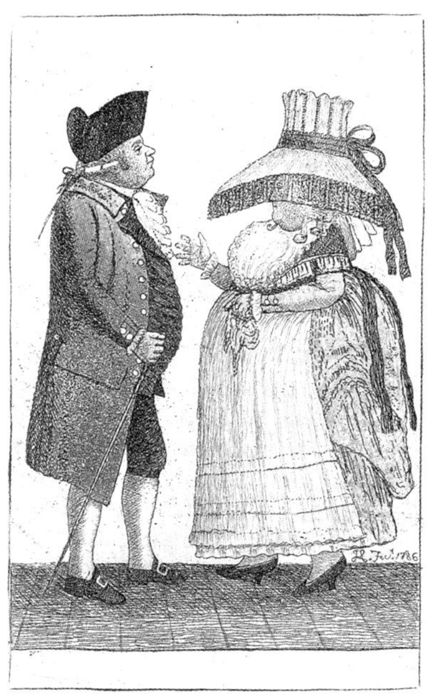

Captain James Justice of Justice Hall, and a lady in the costume of 1790 'The Evening Walk' (1790)

Stepping out on parade

Justice Hall was the family home of Captain Justice in Berwickshire but he often referred to it as Bachelor's Hall on account of his wife having left him. Relating the circumstance of the separation to a friend, he explained that 'Mrs Justice has left me – no matter – she was a good sort of person for all that – a little hot-tempered – only three days after marriage, a leg of mutton made to fly at my head; never mind – plenty of wine, eggs, at Bachelor's Hall – we can make ourselves merry.'

The lady in the print is not named but she was known as a member of the *beau monde* in the New Town where the Evening Walk or Promenade was a popular pastime.

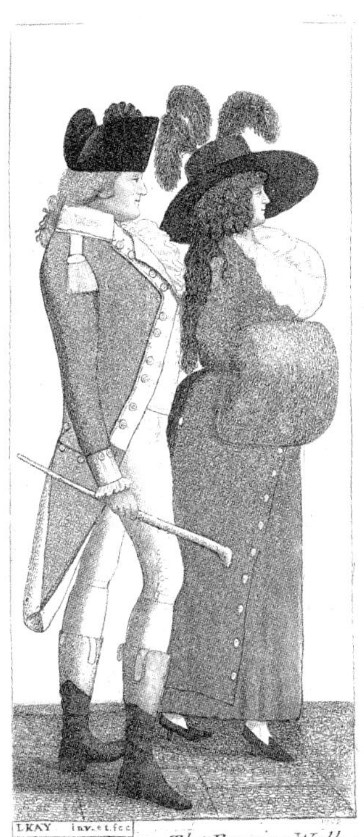

The Evening Walk

Lord Kames, Hugo Arnot of Balcormo, Advocate, Lord Monboddo (1784)

A trio of intellectuals

Kay has put the gaunt figure of Hugo Arnot between Lord Kames and Lord Monboddo, perhaps as a reference to the adversarial relationship that existed between the two intellectuals.

Henry Home, Lord Kames, is best known for his *Elements of Criticism*, published in 1762. When Kames inquired of Lord Monboddo whether he had read his work, he replied, 'I have not, my lord, you write a great deal faster than I am able to read.' Kames was indeed a prolific writer, even dictating notes on his deathbed. When a visitor expressed surprise at this, Kames exclaimed: 'Would you have me stay with my tongue in my cheek till death comes to fetch me?'

His great adversary, James Burnett, Lord Monboddo, was a forerunner in evolutionary theory development, suggesting that humans had evolved from apes and that babies were born with tails. It was said he tried to confirm his tail theory at the births of his own children but each time the supposed evidence disappeared with the midwife. Known also for his eccentric ways, he once walked home in the rain after sending his wig ahead in his sedan chair to keep it dry. One of his favourite foods was a boiled egg and he often commented: 'Show me any of your French cooks who can make a dish like this.' No doubt the menu was more extensive at his 'learned suppers' attended by Professors Black, Hutton and Hope as well as Boswell, Johnson and Burns.

Hugo Arnot is best known for his *History of Edinburgh* published in 1779. Ill health dogged him constantly and on one occasion the bawling of a man selling sand on the streets caused him to lament, 'The rascal! He spends as much breath in a minute as would serve me for a month!'

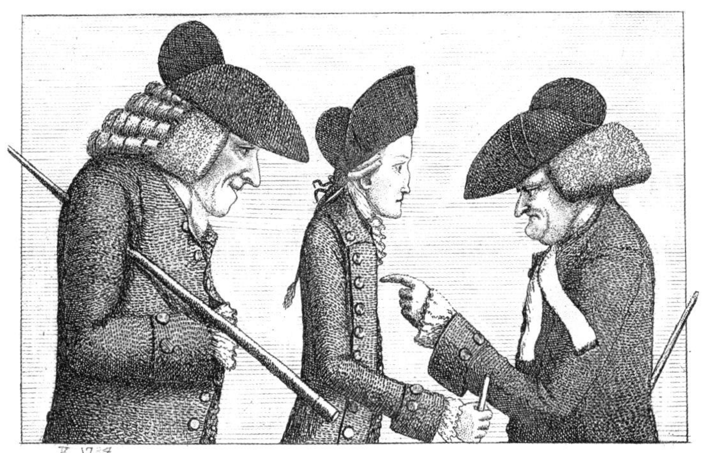

John Kay (1786)

Self-portrait with cat

'He cared for no employment except that of etching likenesses,' Kay's widow once reported.

In this print Kay describes himself as 'sitting in a thoughtful posture in an antiquated chair (whereby he means to represent his love of antiquities) with his favourite cat (the largest it is believed in Scotland) sitting upon the back of it: several pictures hanging behind him; a bust of Homer, with his painting utensils on the table before him, a scroll of paper in his hand, and a volume of his works upon his knee.'

There is no known published work by Kay at this time. It is likely that Kay was keen to publish his work and he may have produced the self-portrait in anticipation of achieving this.

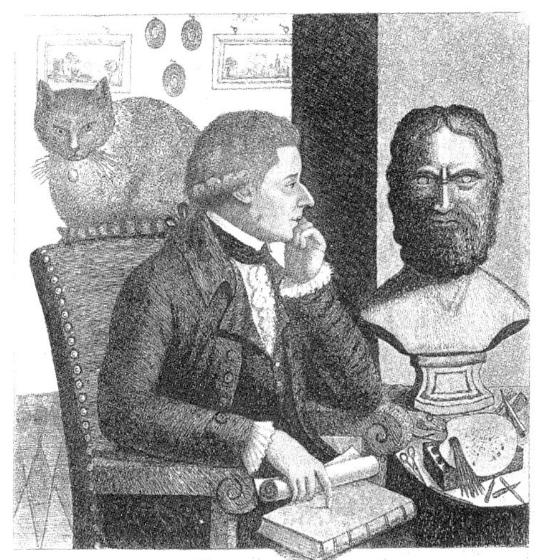

JOHN KAY

Drawn & Engraved by Himself 1786.

Lawyer and Client (1790)

Two sides to every story

This is one of Kay's best-known 'topsy turvy' or ambiguous prints. Kay's shop was close to the law courts so the legal profession is well represented in his work.

Much of the intercourse between lawyers and clients took place in one of the many taverns or coffee houses around Parliament Square and the last item on the legal invoice presented to the client was usually the tavern bill.

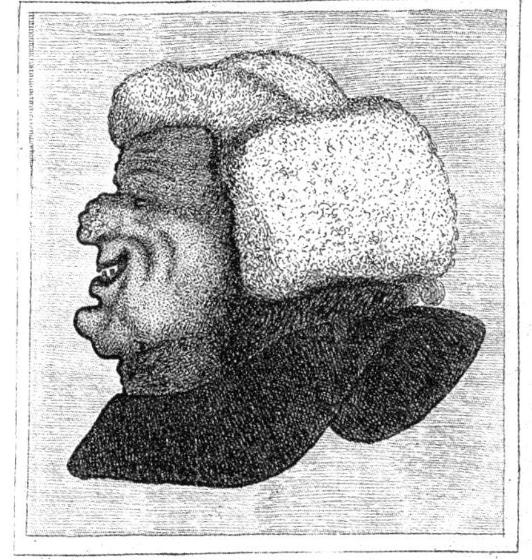

THE LAWYER 1790

Levelling of the
High Street of Edinburgh (1785)

A civic squabble

A plan to level the High Street was put forward by Lord Provost, Sir James Hunter Blair (*LIV*) in 1785. At first it appeared to be a case of simply levelling the 'crown o' the causey' but when it emerged that some parts of the street were to be lowered by up to five feet, opposition grew and an injunction or bill of suspension was passed. Kay could not resist committing the key players in the 'squabble' to paper.

The supporters of the plan are to the fore, first being Orlando Hart, a shoemaker on the High Street and a member of the Town Council. He had the distinction of building 6 Charlotte Square, now Bute House, on land that he bought for £290 in 1792.

William Jamieson, in the centre, was responsible for the public drains of the city of Edinburgh. At an approximate cost of £100,000, all the rubbish was carted to Portobello, an area where Jamieson had extensive lands.

Archibald M'Dowall, to the right, a clothier and leading member of the Council, is seen holding a copy of the disputed plan.

In the background Provost Hunter Blair is portrayed digging up the earth while Thomas Hay, Deacon of the Surgeons, a strong 'anti-leveller' and leader of the opposition in the Council is busy shovelling it in again.

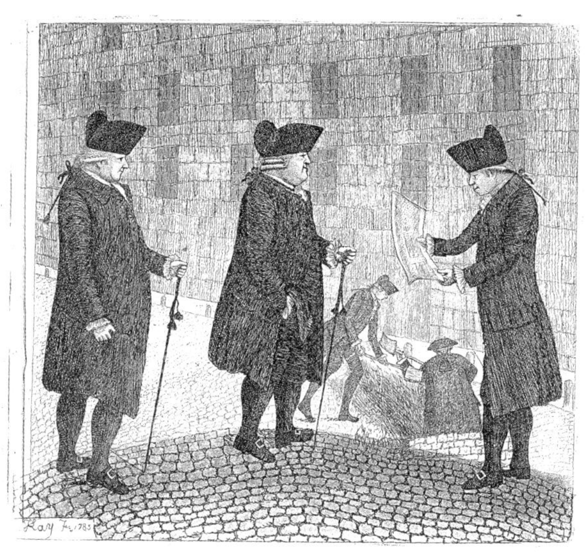

The Lovers (no date)

It is seldom a smooth course

This undated caricature of Captain Dalrymple and Miss Macdonald is supposedly a retaliatory production, the artist's usual method of apologising to those who happened to be offended by his choice of subject. Another etching shows Miss Penelope Macdonald with a Captain Dalrymple, later Sir Robert, wearing the 'fashions prevailing in the *beau monde*' but it does not appear to give offence. It may, however, have upset his wife, Grahame, daughter of Colonel Hepburn of Keith, whom he married in 1800. Miss Macdonald had married William Hamilton of Wishaw in 1789.

Much more offensive at this time might have been the publication of *Ranger's Impartial List of the Ladies of Pleasure in Edinburgh* which was published anonymously in 1775 detailing some fifty of Edinburgh's ladies of pleasure, complete with map. James 'Balloon' Tytler was mooted as the author but strongly denied any connection with what he called a 'dirty, nasty book'.

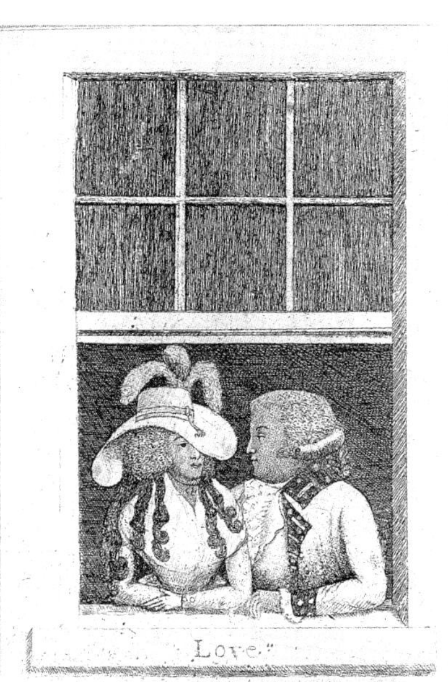

Love."

Vincent Lunardi, in his basket, ready to ascend (1785)

The fashionable balloonist

Kay did this print soon after Lunardi's first successful flight from Heriot's Green, Edinburgh on 5 October 1785. It was a grand occasion, causing shops to close and drawing an audience of some 80,000 to watch the debonair young Italian in his scarlet uniform with blue facings rise into the sky above the city (*see also III*).

Unlike the flight of the hapless Scotsman, 'Balloon' Tytler a few weeks earlier, Lunardi's first ascent in London caused a public sensation. There were rumours of bets of an obscene nature being taken by club members at Brooks as to what could and could not be done in the basket of a balloon, while ladies adopted balloon-shaped hats, known as 'Lunardi bonnets' and wore 'Lunardi skirts' decorated with balloon motifs. Even Burns could not resist a reference in *To A Louse*: 'But Miss's fine Lunardi, fye.'

In Glasgow the silk balloon was exhibited in the choir of St Mungo's cathedral for the admission charge of one shilling. Then on 23 November 1785 Lunardi took off in it from St Andrew's Square, in front of 100,000 spectators, landing near Hawick in the Borders two hours later, at the feet of some 'trembling shepherds'.

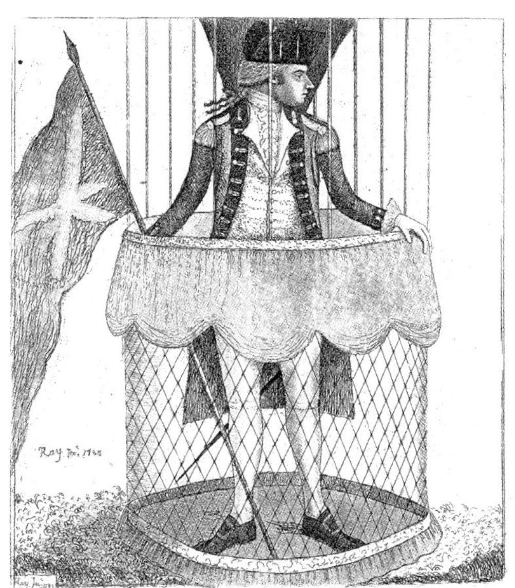

Allan Macdougall of Glenlochan, Alexander Watson of Glenturkie and Colquhoun Grant (1783)

Out for a dram

This is one Kay's earliest prints and features three well-known 'social friends', all Writers to the Signet.

Allan Macdougall, on the left, owned the estate of Glenlochan in Argyllshire but latterly lived in Tweeddale Court on the High Street. The central figure, Alexander Watson of Glenturkie in Fifeshire, was known as a convivial character and lived in Craig's Close, where he had William Smellie, the celebrated engraver and printer, as a neighbour.

To the fore is Colquhoun Grant, brother of Dr Gregory Grant (*XLVII*) and the inseparable companion of Watson. These two bachelors dined daily in the house of Thomas Sommers, a vintner in Jackson's Close who considered them frugal on account of their having only a half bottle of claret between them!

The three gentlemen are portrayed here walking out to the country, which was a popular pastime when rules regarding drinking on the Sabbath were relaxed. This encouraged city dwellers to leave the High Street taverns and the words below mention some of their destinations.

Newhaven, Leith or Canonmills
Supply them in their Sunday gills.
Where writers often spend their pence,
To stock their head wi' drink and sense.

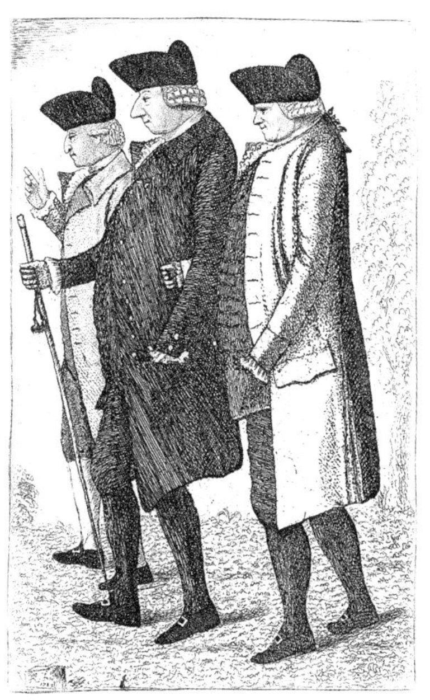

The Rev. Joseph Robertson Macgregor, First Minister of the Edinburgh Gaelic Chapel (1789)

Cleric to the Highlanders

When the Old Gaelic Chapel on Castlehill was erected in 1769, the Reverend Joseph Macgregor became its first minister. He was also chaplain to the 3rd (Highland) Royal Edinburgh Volunteers when they formed in 1797. Both officers and men of the regiment wore a red, white and green-diced hummel bonnet decorated with black feathers, red coats and dark blue pantaloons. Most of the 400 members of the regiment were Highlanders living and working in Edinburgh.

Macgregor had previously been known as Joseph Robertson, having chosen his mother's surname after the name Macgregor was proscribed. On repeal of the Proscriptive Act he took back his proper name of Macgregor.

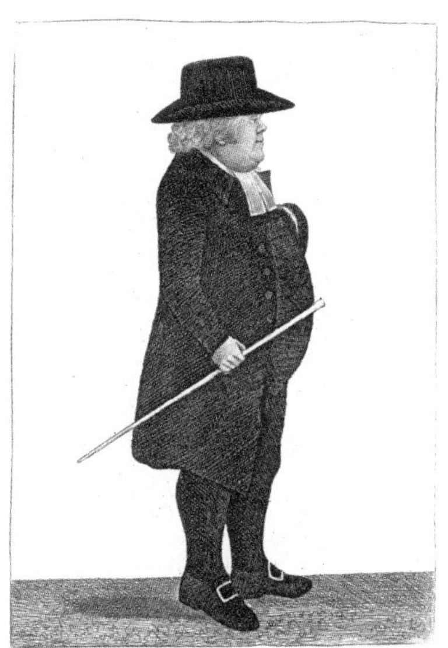

Hugh Macpherson, sometime Clerk to the Perth Carriers (1810)

A determined dandy

'Wee Hughie' grew up in the Highlands but moved to Perth and finally settled in Edinburgh a year or two before the publication of Kay's print of 1810.

Employed with Messrs J. and P. Cameron, carriers between Perth and Edinburgh, Hugh Macpherson considered himself 'a perfect dandy' and soon abandoned his highland garb for a dark green coat, light vest, darkish trousers and high-heeled boots.

His odd figure and self-conceit assured his notoriety but 'Wee Hughie' was at his most vulnerable in front of females. Once when dancing with great gusto at a ball he was tripped up by a mischievous participator in the reel. Wee Hughie was furious and hurled a candlestick at his mocker. On other occasions the slightest smile or glance from a female was taken for much more that it really was and often led to embarrassment.

'Wee Hughie' enjoyed the conviviality of drinking and one night he left a tavern on the South Bridge to complete an errand. On return, whether on account of the darkness or his alcoholic state, he walked straight into an empty hogshead lying on its side at the tavern door. Failing to find a door handle he rattled the end of the hogshead so vigorously with his cane that he not only roused his friends but the police to boot. It was an episode that was recalled time and time again, much to his indignation.

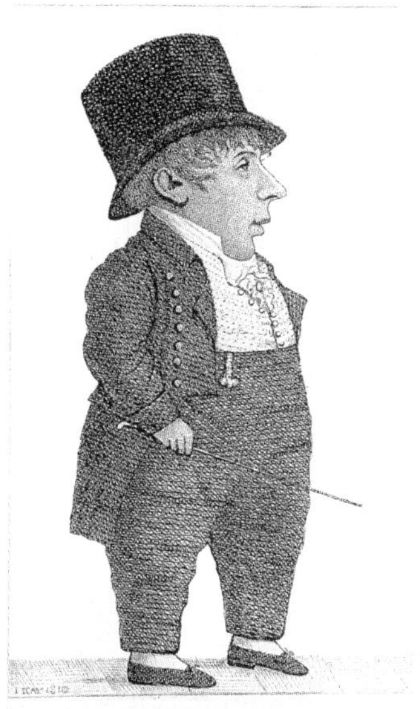

Marriage (1789)

A topsy-turvy affair

Less than 350 people sued for divorce in the Commissary Court of Edinburgh in the eighteenth century and almost a quarter of these involved husbands who were soldiers or merchants. With a population of around 1.6 million in Scotland in 1800, this divorce statistic seems to indicate little marital conflict in eighteenth-century Scotland.

Kay's print, viewed the other way round after rotation through 180 degrees, suggests that the reality may have been quite different!

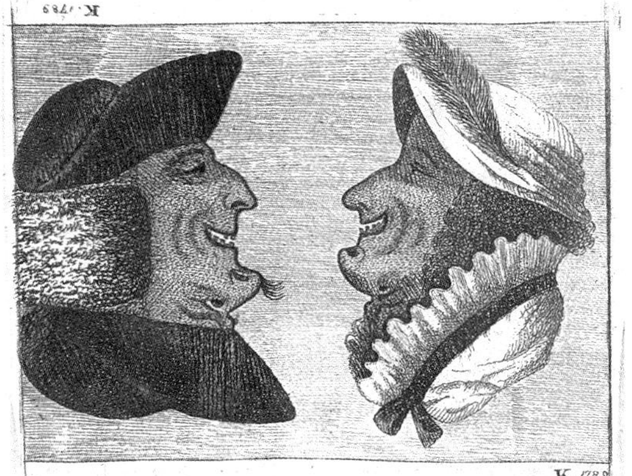
AFTER MARRIAGE
K. 1789
BEFORE MARRIAGE
K. 1789

Lauchlan M'Bain (1791)

Roasting-jack seller and Culloden veteran

Lauchlan M'Bain was a well-kent face around the old Parliament Square. He survived Culloden, but with no pension forthcoming, he set up in Edinburgh as a seller of fly-jacks and toasting forks. He was 'the author of all he made, said or sang' and would announce his arrival in the Parliament Close with the chant quoted here in Kay's print.

> Now for your quarters and Shoulders of Mutton
>> or Lamb, Geese or turkeys.
> Any more a Wanting my hearty ones.
> What! are you all asleep, nous your time.
> I leave this City to morrow & have Sold
>> Sixteen Hundred dozen
> All well prov'd, well try'd, the last one now.

This chant however proved to be an irritation to the judges in the Courthouse, especially when M'Bain stood right underneath their window 'to exert his stentorian lungs' and eventually they 'bought' his silence. Respite was short-lived, as M'Bain reappeared at his usual spot ringing a huge bell. When challenged by passers-by as to the new mode of announcing his arrival, he explained that 'having sold his *own* tongue to the judges, he was under the necessity of using another (the bell).' The result was a further payment.

But for all his local fame, fortune escaped the roasting-jack vendor and he ended up in the Charity Workhouse. At the grand age of ninety-six he was expelled for 'an amour', but luckily for him, his new love became his wife and cared for him until his death at the grand old age of 102.

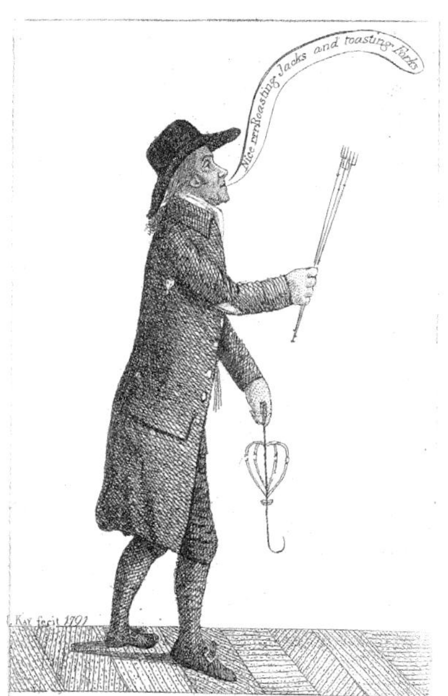

Now for your quarters and Shoulders of Mutton or
Lamb Geese and turkeys. any more a Wanting my
hearty ones. What are you all asleep nous your time.
I leave this City to morrow & have Sold Sixteen
Hundred dozen all well provd well try'd. the last one now

Robert Macgachen,
Accountant of Excise
'Knowing One' (1802)

The business of money

Kay's title, *Knowing One*, has no explanation but it is likely that it refers to the subject's ability with figures. In his early years Macgachen had lost over £10,000 left to him by his father, but perhaps the hard lessons learnt from such a loss made him a better accountant in later life. Kay states that the likeness was commissioned at the request of a person who suggested the title. Perhaps the commissioner had benefited from Mr Macgachen's accounting skills.

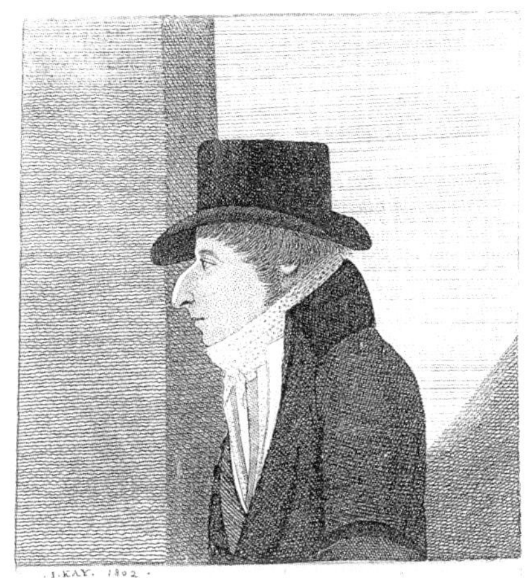

KNOWING ONE.

Captain Mingay, with a Porter Carrying George Cranstoun in his Creel (1784)

Quite overtaken, Geordie is exported home

Captain Mingay was an Irish soldier who came to Edinburgh with his regiment. There is no explanation for his being included in the print.

George Cranstoun (*XVII*) was known as a 'shrewd and intelligent little personage' and an excellent singer of comic songs. He was often placed on the sideboard to entertain a gathering 'of choice spirits' but frequently indulged too much so that a porter would be called to take 'Geordie' home. Kay illustrates the practice with Geordie wedged in a creel, clutching his stick and en route back home to his mother. On one occasion when no creel was available it was said that his hosts wrapped him up as a parcel, marked 'carriage paid' and addressed it to his long-suffering mother.

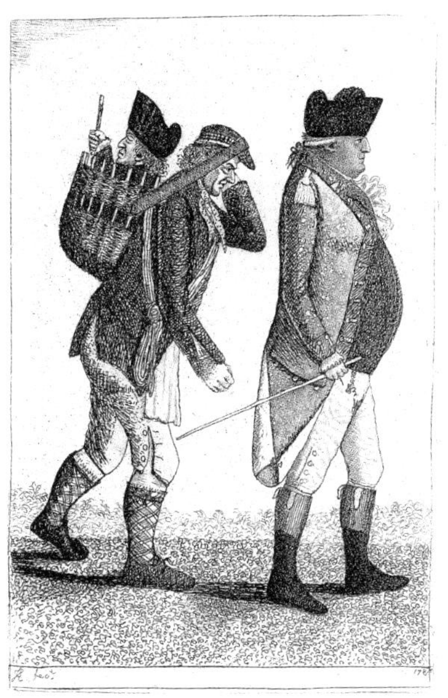

Dr Alexander Monro, Secundus, Professor of Anatomy at the University of Edinburgh (1790)

A man of influence

Three medics, each named Alexander Monro, Primus, Secundus and Tertius, held the Chair of Anatomy consecutively for 126 years at the University of Edinburgh. Alexander Monro Secundus, the subject of Kay's print was considered the greatest of the Monro dynasty and was President of the Royal College of Physicians of Edinburgh from 1779 to 1782.

While anatomy flourished, surgery was tainted with an academic prejudice against what was still perceived as a manual craft rather than an intellectual discipline. In 1766 Alexander Hamilton (*L*) put forward a proposal for a separate Chair of Surgery at the University of Edinburgh with James Rae (*LXXXI*) a strong contender for the post. Monro Secundus blocked the proposal and secured agreement for a combined Chair of Anatomy and Surgery for himself. He and his son delivered surgical lectures despite both being physicians with no surgical training. It was left to Benjamin Bell (*V*) and the brothers John and Charles Bell to establish Edinburgh as a centre of excellence for surgical teaching.

The influence of the Monro dynasty has continued, albeit in a different direction. Charles John Monro, great-grandson of Monro Secundus, is credited with bringing the game of rugby to New Zealand.

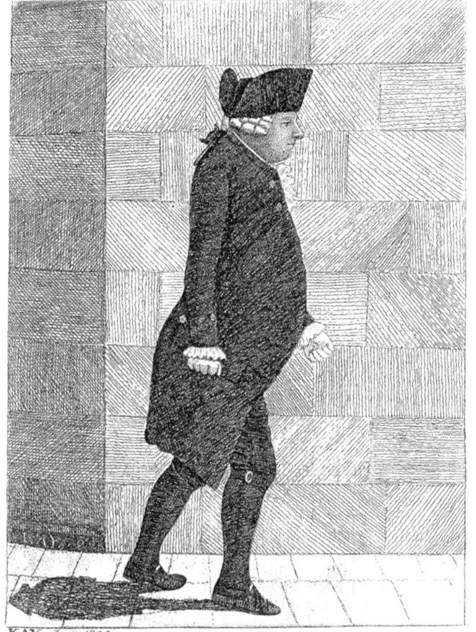
KAY. fecit 1790

Sir James Montgomery of Stanhope and David Stuart Moncrief of Moredun, His Majesty's Barons of Exchequer (1788)

Country lovers

Sir James Montgomery, on the left, held a series of high offices including Solicitor-General for Scotland, Lord Advocate and in 1777, on the death of Lord Chief-Baron Ord, he became Lord Chief-Baron of his Majesty's Court of Exchequer. He was the first Scotsman to hold this office since 1707.

David Stuart Moncrief was a Baron of the Exchequer but devoted much of his time to cultivating his estate at Moredun, south of Edinburgh. Sir James was also keen on agricultural improvements and in Kay's print this may well be the topic of their conversation. Baron Moncrief was a bachelor and intended to pass his estate to his nephew, Sir Thomas Moncrief, Bt, who had married, according to his uncle's wishes, Lady Elizabeth Ramsay, sister of the Earl of Dalhousie. The marriage faltered but the baron blamed his nephew for the discord and duly settled his estate on Lady Elizabeth.

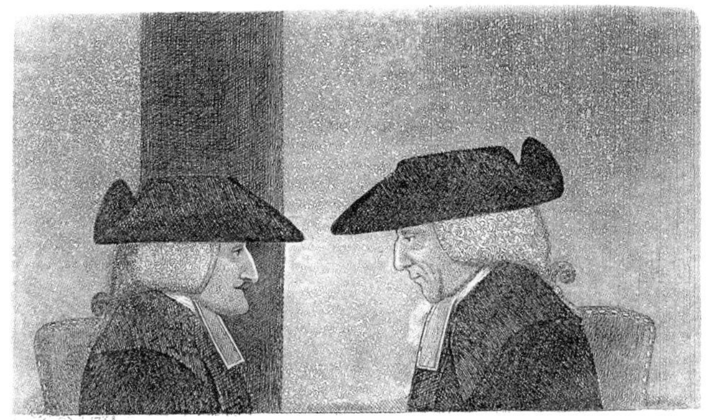

William Wilson or 'Mortar Willie' (1815)

Not the retiring type

This very fine etching of 'Mortar Willie' was done in 1815, the year of his death in Edinburgh. Mortar Willie was born 'within a bow-shot of Castle Huntly'. After thirty years working on a farm he enlisted in the army, fought against the Pretender and then served abroad. On return he worked in a bark-mill in London and then settled in Edinburgh when he was almost seventy years old. He worked for many establishments in the city but for many years was in the employ of Doctor Burt. When Willie became frail and less productive after his hundredth year, the kindly doctor continued to pay his faithful employee his two shillings daily allowance. Willie appreciated the gesture and on days when he achieved little, he would remark to the doctor, 'Eh man, ye've got a bad bargain the day.'

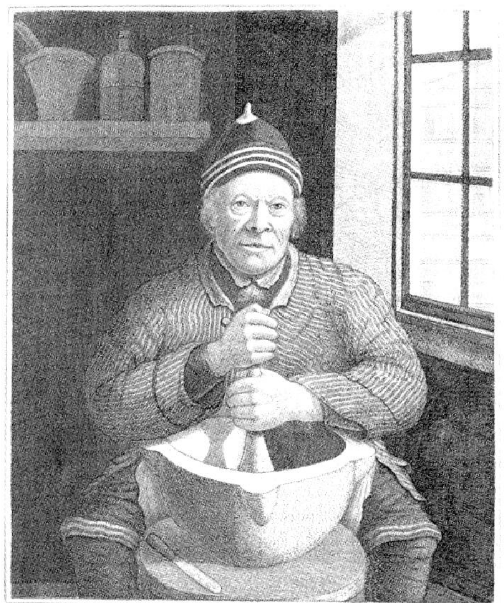

WILL^M WILSON. *Commonly called*
Mortar Willie. Aged. 107.

I KAY 1818

Thomas Muir, Esq.,
Younger of Huntershill (1793)

*Illustrious Martyr in the glorious cause
Of truth, of freedom, and of equal laws.*

Kay is perhaps indicating his own political sentiments in this print of 1793, the year of Muir's trial in Edinburgh. It is certainly meant to present Muir as a learned and accomplished gentleman rather than a convicted seditionist. Given the popularity of Kay's print of Thomas Paine (*LXXVI*), this was probably another bestseller for the artist.

Thomas Muir was born near Glasgow in 1765 and trained as a lawyer. Liberal in politics, he was quick to embrace the sentiments of the French Revolution and was an active member of the Scottish Branch of the Friends of the People. In 1793, in a highly politicised trial before Lord Braxfield (*XII*) and a handpicked jury of anti-reformers, Muir was found guilty of exciting a spirit of disloyalty and disaffection, of recommending and distributing Paine's *The Rights of Man* and of seditious writing. He was transported to Botany Bay but escaped and finally arrived in France in 1797. He was made a French citizen and died at Chantilly, near Paris, in 1799.

Muir is the first name on the Martyrs' Monument in the Old Calton Burial Ground in Edinburgh, which was erected by the friends of parliamentary reform in England and Scotland in 1844.

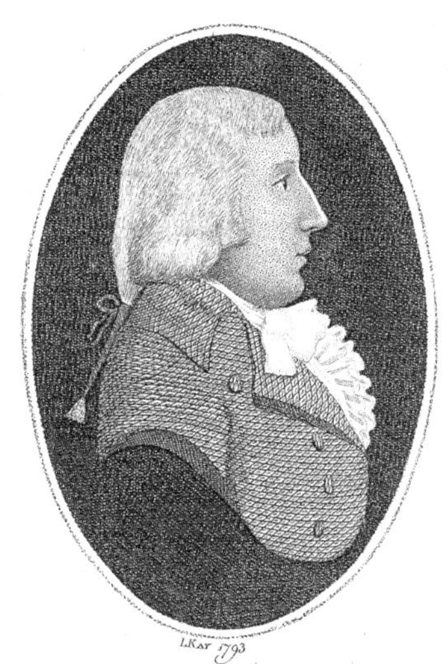

Illustrious Martyr in the glorious cause
Of truth, of freedom, and of equal laws.

Thomas Paine, Secretary for Foreign Affairs to the American Colonies (no date)

A radical propagandist

Kay had relatives in America and this likeness was made from a miniature sent to him around 1794. Given the publicity surrounding Paine's controversial writings, Kay obviously saw the potential for selling prints and this one became a bestseller.

Although Paine never visited Edinburgh, his works were widely read and *The Rights of Man* was even translated into Gaelic. One of the charges against Thomas Muir (*LXXV*), the 'Scottish Martyr', was distributing and recommending Thomas Paine's radical work *The Rights of Man*. Burns, too, was inspired by it and in 1792 produced the prologue *The Rights of Woman* for Miss Louise Fontenelle's Benefit Night, the title echoing Paine's revolutionary work and quoting the line:

'And even children lisp the Rights of Man'

Given the impact of his writings it is interesting to note that Paine never established a political society or organization and was not directly responsible for a single reforming measure. He did not even speak French and had his works translated and read for him after joining the French National Assembly in 1792.

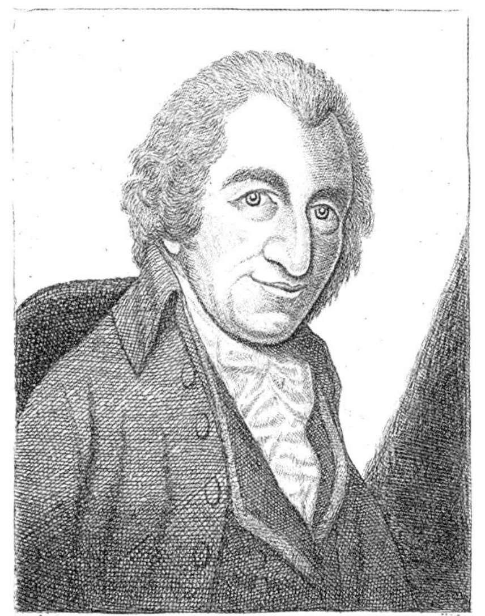

THOMAS PAINE.

Petticoat Government, or the Gray Mare is the Better Horse (1795)

The woman behind the man

When the government sanctioned the raising of Fencible regiments in 1793, John Campbell, 1st Marquis of Breadalbane raised 2,300 men of whom 1,600 were from the Breadalbane estates around Kenmore. This print, when published in 1795, caused quite a stir, especially amongst the Breadalbane Fencibles, who were stationed in Edinburgh at that time. No names were given but the subjects were deemed to be Lord and Lady Breadalbane. It was said that the idea for the print was suggested to Kay by a few disgruntled officers of the Fencibles, who, having been refused leave of absence, attributed their want of success to the interference of Lady Breadalbane.

Breadalbane's great achievement was the building of Taymouth Castle, begun in 1806. The central block and tower, the so-called 'Tea Cadie' was said to be 'more than a passing reference' to the rival Campbell seat at Inveraray. The extensive western block was designed by James Gillespie Graham and completed in 1834, while assistance with the interiors came from his friend and colleague, A. W. N. Pugin.

There is no evidence to show that Lord Breadalbane was not his own master or that his wife held any undue sway over him. Indeed a notable feature in the grounds of Taymouth is a memorial cross, erected at great expense by Breadalbane in 1831, in honour of his wife.

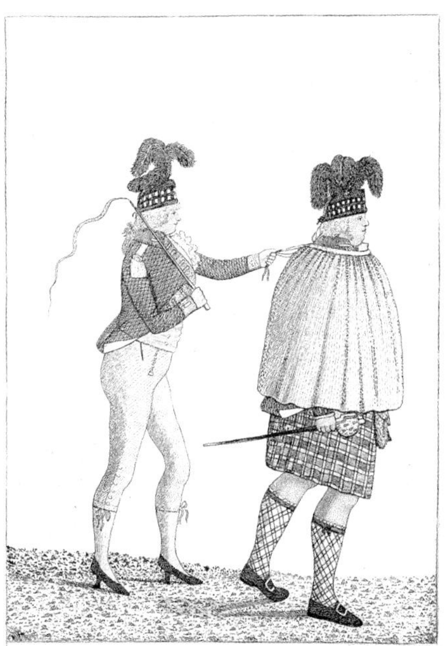

PETTICOAT GOVERNMENT
or
the Gray mare is the Better Horse.

Philosophers (1787)

Two great minds, Joseph Black and James Hutton

Kay's print conveys the close friendship of Black (*VIII*) and Hutton (*LV*) and it was often noted how they could converse at long length without any awareness of what was going on around them. On one occasion they set out to find premises for a literary meeting and summoned their intellectual friends to a venue on the South Bridge. Hutton arrived late and noted the presence of several 'well-dressed but somewhat brazen faced young ladies' in an adjoining room. It seems the bachelor philosophers had managed to choose one of the most noted houses of 'ill fame' for their meeting!

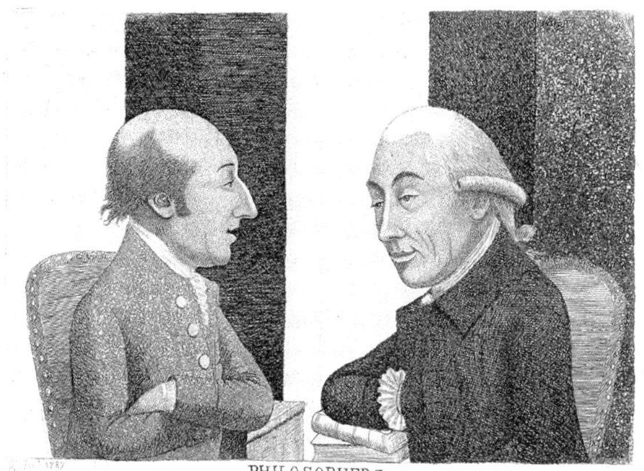
PHILOSOPHERS

Mr Pierie and Mr Maxwell (1785)

Confirmed bachelors

The Ladies are in the costume of 1785. Mr Pierie and Mr Maxwell were bachelors and perhaps Kay is alluding to this by placing the rather plain and portly gentlemen alongside three of the most fashionable ladies of the day.

Nothing is known of Mr Maxwell but Mr Pierie, on the left, was Extractor of the King's Processes in the Court of Session. He was also a member of the Crochallan Fencibles, one of the city's most convivial drinking clubs founded by William Smellie (*LXXXVI*) in 1778, so he would have known Adam Smith (*LXXXVII*), Hugh Blair, Henry Mackenzie and Lord Monboddo (*LIX*). As Maxwell died on 24 July 1786, he did not get to meet Smellie's autumn recruit, one Robert Burns, who arrived in Edinburgh on 28 November that same year.

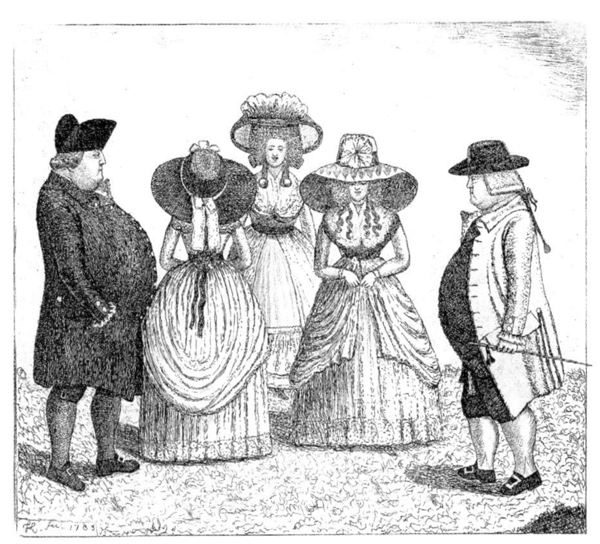

William Pitt (1800)

The younger statesman

Kay visited London in 1800 and the likeness of Pitt the Younger is one of the few portraits that he created while there (*see also XVIII*). Pitt never once set foot in Scotland but perhaps there was no need with the indomitable Henry Dundas (*XVIII, XXXI*) taking care of his interests north of the border.

Pitt's administration was the subject of much satire, notable in *The Rolliad*, which was originally published in serial form in the *Morning Herald* from 1784 to 1785. One topic for ridicule was his youth, with *The Rolliad* declaring,

> A sight to make surrounding nations stare
> A kingdom trusted to a schoolboy's care!

While regarded as an accomplished orator in Parliament, Pitt was not known for his witty remarks but he did deliver a quick retort on one occasion. When one of the London Corporations offered to set up a Volunteer Corps on condition of its never being sent abroad, Pitt agreed with them, saying, 'I will engage that they shall never leave the country, except in case of an invasion.'

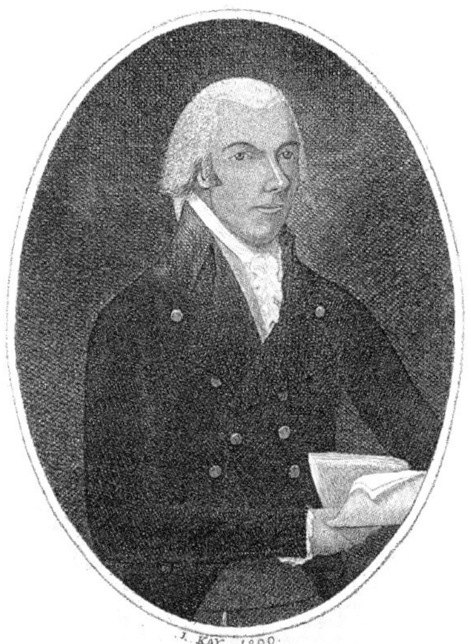
J. KAY. 1800.

James Rae, Dr William Laing and Dr James Hay (1786)

A visionary teacher

James Rae is first figure on left, with Dr William Laing and his niece in the centre and James Hay, army surgeon and latterly Inspector of the Military Ward at the Royal Infirmary of Edinburgh, on the right. It was a popular custom for people to meet at the Cross on Edinburgh's High Street between one and two o'clock in the afternoon and Kay may well have seen this group as he walked between his home on the High Street and his print shop in Parliament Square.

James Rae is the best known of the group. Edinburgh was well established as a world centre for medical education and credit is due to James Rae for the establishment of systematic clinical teaching at the Royal Infirmary of Edinburgh and the first planned course of lectures in surgery at Surgeon's Hall in High School Yards.

In 1766 when a proposal was put forward by Alexander Hamilton (*L*) for a separate Chair of Surgery at the University, Rae would have been the strongest contender for the post. However Alexander Monro, Secundus (*LXXII*), who held the Chair of Anatomy, blocked the proposal and in due course benefited from his counter proposal, which gave him the new title of Professor of Anatomy and Surgery – a real coup given that Monro, Secundus was not a surgeon.

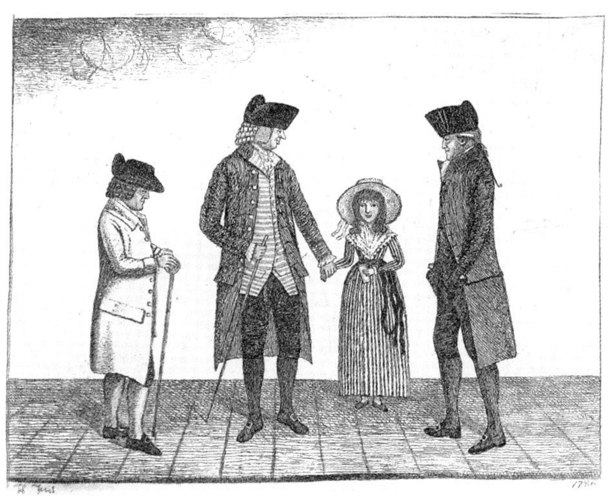

Lord Rockville, Dr Adam Smith and Commissioner George Brown (1787)

A chance encounter

Adam Smith (*LXXXVII*) is seen here in the centre with a fellow Commissioner of Excise, George Brown to the right. George was the brother of James Brown, the architect of Brown's Square, previously sited on the west side of Chambers Street, Edinburgh. He also designed George Square a little further to the south, which he named after his brother George, not George III as some have suggested.

Alexander Gordon, Lord Rockville, shown on the left, was a member of the Crochallan Fencibles and arrived on one occasion to relate a strange experience to his fellow members: 'As I was walking along the Grassmarket, all of a sudden the street rose up and struck me in the face!' It was soon realised that Lord Rockville had been paying too much homage to Bacchus and had slipped and fallen on his way up to the High Street.

Ironically he died after a fall at his home at St Andrew Square in the New Town in 1792.

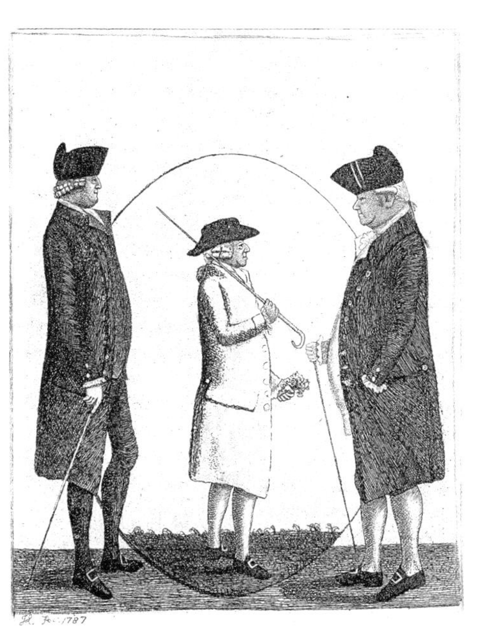
1787

David Ross, Lord Ankerville (1799)

Connoisseur of claret

David Ross of Inverchasely was born in 1727 and admitted to the bar in 1751. He was promoted to the bench as Lord Ankerville in 1776 and set up home at 3 St Andrew Square, Edinburgh.

Lord Ankerville was best known for enjoying the 'pleasures of the table' and for preferring claret to whisky. Whenever he made his annual trip to his estate at Tarlogie, near Tain in Ross-shire he was always fastidious in having innkeepers along his route forewarned of the need for decent claret. On one occasion when disturbed at dinner at his Highland seat, Invercharron House, by a visitor, he apologised for his uncropped beard but insisted that his guest sit with him and enjoy the best of Highland hospitality. After an ample amount of food and quite a few glasses of his best claret, Lord Ankerville excused himself and returned in due course sporting a very closely shaved visage. The judge advised the astonished guest that his hand was now much more steady than it would have been in the morning.

Lord Ankerville was Provost of Tain, three times the Master of Lodge St Duthus and in 1809 donated the land for the building of the new Tain Academy.

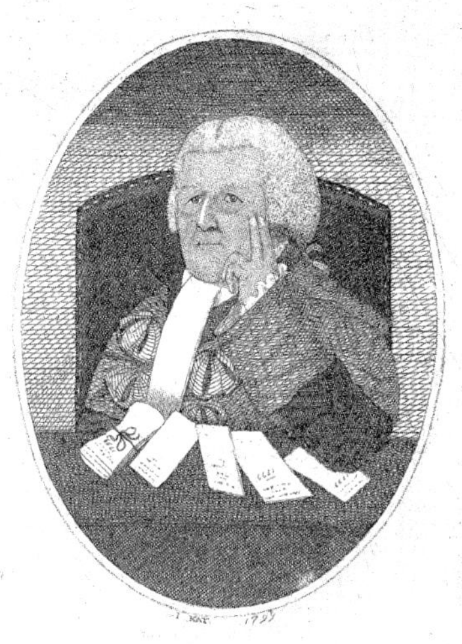

Ralph Rylance (1813)

Universal penman and indexer of The Edinburgh Review

Ralph Rylance came to Scotland only once, in 1813. The purpose of his visit was to supervise the compilation of the Index to the first twenty volumes of *The Edinburgh Review* and it was his publisher and friend, Archibald Constable, who commissioned Kay to produce this print.

Rylance also worked for Longman & Co, and was known for his linguistic skills and fluency in eighteen languages. His comments in *The Morning Chronicle* on Sir Walter Scott's *The Field of Waterloo* are perhaps less known:

> The corps of many a hero slain
> Graced Waterloo's ensanguined plain;
> But none, by sabre, or by shot,
> Fell half so flat as Walter Scott!

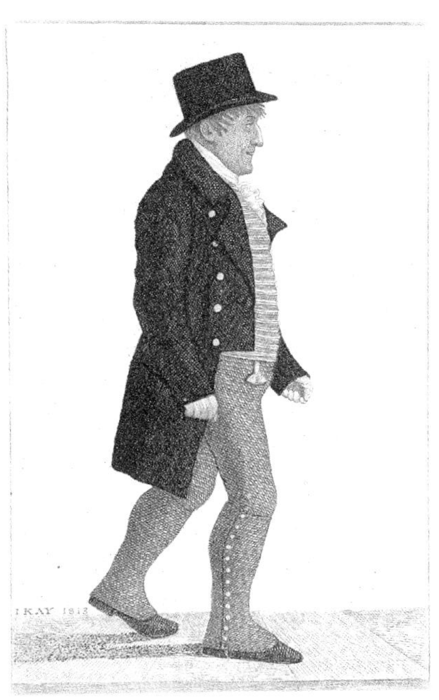
KAY 1813

Sir John Sinclair of Ulbster (1791)

The Scottish patriot

While James Gillray, the political and social satirist, mocked Sir John Sinclair in contemporary prints, Kay presents him as the upright young patriotic reformer.

Known as 'Agricultural Sir John' because of his interest in agricultural improvements and many years of service to the Board of Agriculture, Sir John's greatest achievement was the completion of the *First Statistical Account of Scotland*, published as twenty-one volumes over eight years, from 1791. It was the first use of the term 'statistics', which Sir John explained thus: 'the idea I annex to the term is an inquiry into the state of a country, for the purpose of ascertaining the quantum of happiness enjoyed by its inhabitants, and the means of its future improvement'.

Sir John was one of the first to wear Highland dress after the law banning it was repealed in 1782. On seeing Sinclair in full Highland costume, one local on his Caithness estate assured him that if he had 'come in the good old cause, there were a hundred gude men ready to join him within the sound o' the Bell o' Logierait'.

In his last years Sir John lived at 133 George Street in Edinburgh, the local name for the pavement in front of this house being the Giants' Causeway, since each member of his family, including himself, exceeded six feet in height.

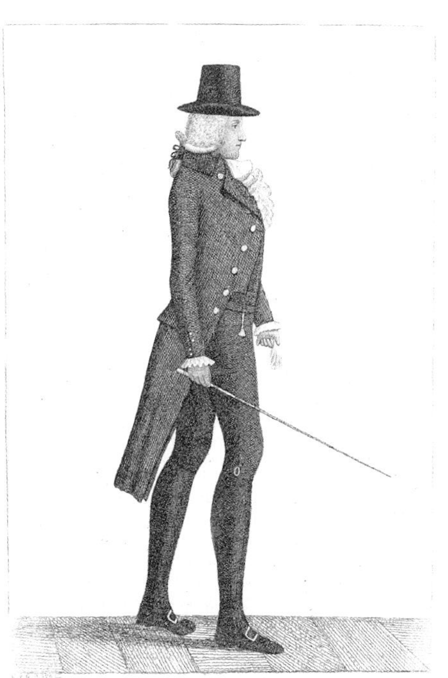

The Scottish Patriot.

William Smellie, Printer, FRS FAS and Andrew Bell, Engraver (1787)

A good nose for story

Andrew Bell's tiny body and enormous nose made him a desirable subject for caricature. He often mocked himself and sported an artificial nose, 'to the inexpressible horror and amazement of those who were not aware of the trick'. Bell was for many years the proprietor of the *Encyclopaedia Britannica*. His good friend William Smellie was editor of the first edition, published in 1771.

Alongside his reputation as a scholar printer, Smellie was an accomplished naturalist and antiquary, with his *Philosophy of Natural History* drawing an offer of 1000 guineas for the copyright from Mr C. Elliot before a single page was written! He was a good friend of the poet Burns, who described him as 'one of the best hearts and keenest wits that I have ever met with', and introduced him to the Crochallan Fencibles, a club he helped set up in facetious imitation of the local Volunteer Corps, and which met at Douglas's Tavern in Anchor Close.

Smellie was a golfer and famous for taking up a bet in 1798 at the Burgess Golfing Society that no two members could drive a ball from the south-east corner of Parliament Square over the spire of St Giles. Along with another member, the feat was achieved with the balls easily clearing the spire and landing opposite Advocate's Close on the north side of the High Street.

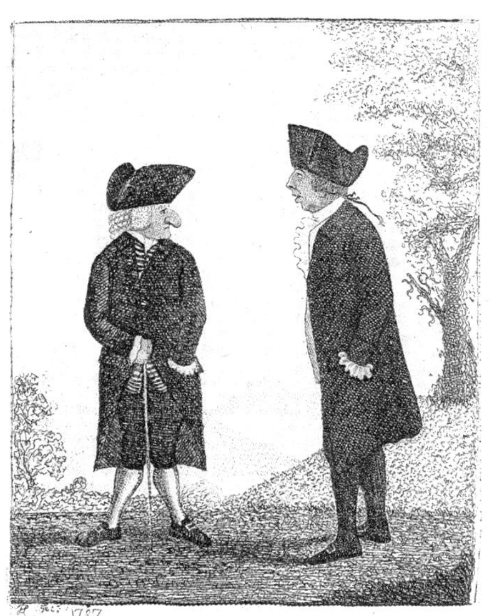

Adam Smith LLD and FRS
of London and Edinburgh (1790)

Father of modern economics

The print shows Smith (*see also LXXXII*) with *The Wealth of Nations*, on the desk beside him. It is often described as the only known likeness of Smith to be done in his lifetime but James Tassie's medallion in the Scottish National Portrait Gallery is dated 1787, three years before Smith's death. At the time of writing his image lives on as the first Scotsman to feature on a Bank of England £20 note.

Although he spent his latter years as a Commissioner of Excise in Edinburgh, Smith travelled extensively and met with many of the great European thinkers, including Voltaire, Turgot, Quesnay and Necker. At home his intellectual circle included Joseph Black (*VIII*) and James Hutton (*LV*), both executors of his will and diligent in carrying out Smith's instructions to destroy most of his manuscripts and writings, much to the chagrin of later historians and biographers.

Smith was a member of many clubs including the Glasgow Literary Society, the Political Economy Society of Glasgow, as well as the Select Society, the Oyster Club and the Poker Club in Edinburgh. He entertained extensively at Panmure House, his home in the Canongate, but was also an honoured guest at many fine tables. Arriving late for a dinner once in London with Henry Dundas, later Lord Melville (*XVIII, XXXI*), the dinner guests who included Mr Pitt, Mr Addington, Mr Grenville all stood up to greet the latecomer and when Smith entreated them to sit down, the reply was: 'No, we will stand till you are seated, for we are all your scholars.'

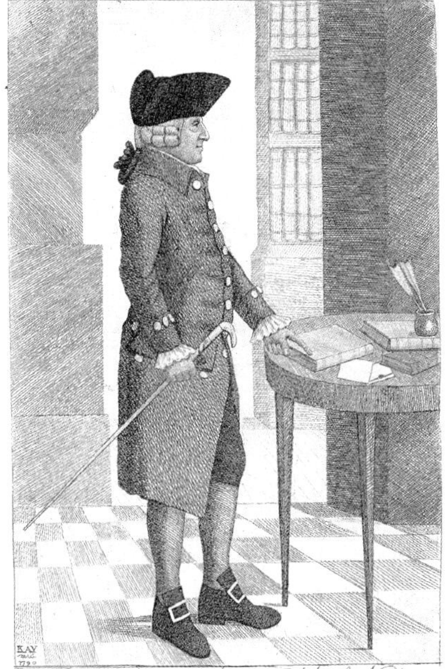

The Author of the Wealth of Nations

George Smith and Deacon William Brodie
'The First Interview in 1786' (1788)

A vile encounter

Deacon Brodie's penchant for gambling is alluded to in Kay's print with the inclusion of the dog and cockerel. Claimed to be the inspiration for Stevenson's *Strange Tale of Dr Jekyll and Mr Hyde*, Deacon Brodie led a double life. A respectable Deacon of the Wrights and Masons by day, he transformed himself into a burglar by night.

The first interview with George Smith took place in 1786, when Brodie recruited him along with two others, Brown and Ainslie as accomplices. Brodie's downfall came with the failure of his plan to rob the Excise Office in Chessel's Court in the Canongate. When captured, Ainslie agreed to turn King's evidence in order to avoid transportation. Brodie escaped to the Netherlands in the hope of getting to the United States but was arrested in Amsterdam and brought back to Edinburgh for trial. Smith and Brodie were found guilty and hanged at the Tolbooth on 1 October 1788, apparently on the same gallows that Brodie had designed and funded a year earlier.

Another 'Jekyll and Hyde' aspect of Brodie's life was his fondness for gambling with the lower orders at Clark's in the Fleshmarket Close after enjoying the conviviality of the Cape Club, where his illustrious fellow members included Sir Henry Raeburn, Robert Fergusson and John Rennie, architect of London Bridge and the bridge over the Tweed at Kelso.

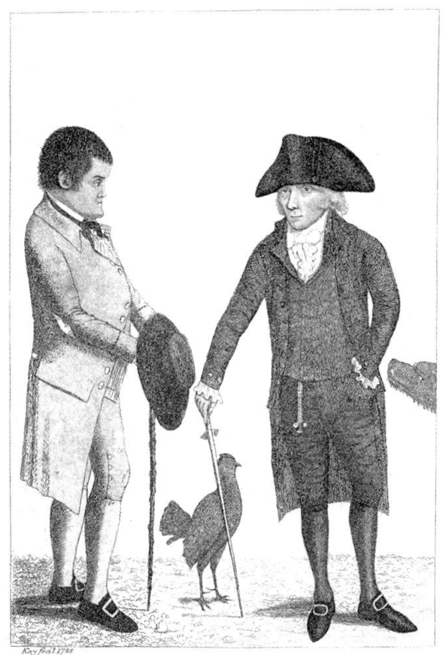

The First Interview in 1786

Provost David Steuart
and Bailie John Lothian (1784)

The great literacy divide

The contrasting figures of the Provost and the Bailie are well defined in this early print by Kay. Bailie Lothian's stoop and round shoulders earned him the nickname, 'The Loupin-on-Stane'.

David Steuart was a banker and later a merchant in Edinburgh. He was elected Lord Provost in 1780 and in 1785 was one of the founders of the Edinburgh Chamber of Commerce. A passionate book collector, Steuart's library was one of the finest in Scotland. Some of his rarest volumes, including a Gutenberg Bible and a Breviary printed in Venice by Nicolaus Jenson in 1478, were to pass to the Library of the Faculty of Advocates, now part of the National Library of Scotland.

John Lothian was a cloth-merchant on the High Street and became a bailie in 1768. Unlike Provost Steuart, he had little taste for literature and no aptitude for languages.

When invited to a funeral service by William Smellie (*LXXXVI*), the famous Edinburgh printer, he was unable to decipher the order of service on account of it being in Latin. He decided that Mr Smellie had in fact given him a libellous document berating himself and the civic authorities so he presented it at the next Council meeting. Everyone present could see what the document really was, and Bailie Lothian had to suffer the embarrassment of the raucous laughter that ensued.

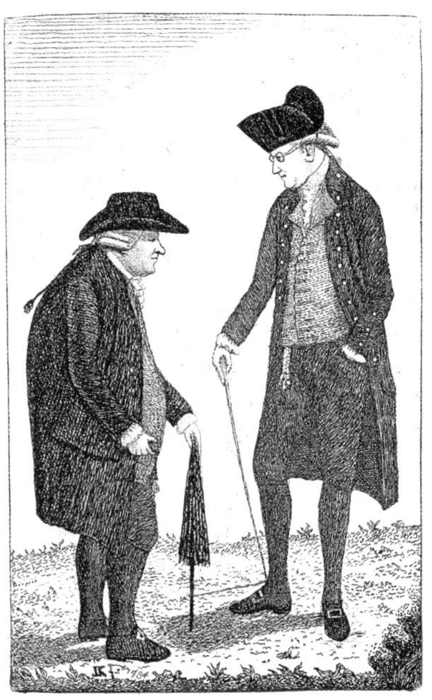

Margaret Suttie,
a Hawker of Salt (1799)

Saut Maggie

Like her mother before her, Margaret made her living from selling salt in Edinburgh. She purchased her daily supply at either Pinkie or Joppa and then carried her consignment back into the Old Town. As with fish, the traditional hawkers of salt were female.

'Wha'll buy my lucky forpit o' sa-at – Na Na, deil ane yet!' was Margaret's usual cry with her use of the word 'lucky' meaning a generous measure. She was best known to the locals for her habit of talking out loud and of making unfortunate remarks. While walking down the Canongate she noticed a rather corpulent clergyman waddling ahead of her. 'Eh but he's fat – see how he shugs! Wha'll buy my lucky forpit o' sa-at – see how he shugs!'

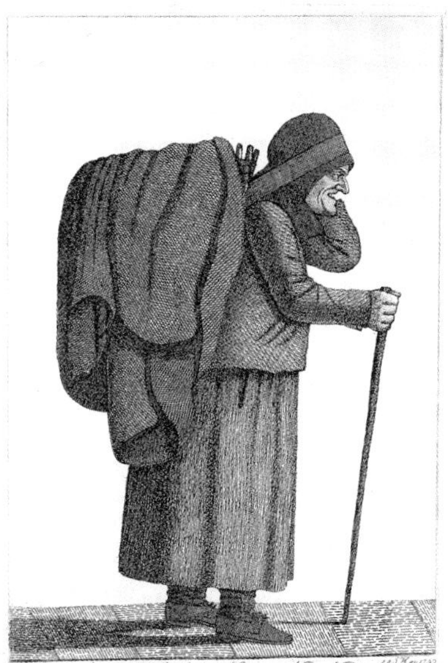

Wha'l buy my lucky forpit o' Sa.a't. Na: Na: it 'ill nae dee:
Deel ane yet.

Old Geordie Syme,
a Famous Piper in his Time (1789)

Tunes for all occasions

Old Geordie Syme was a well-respected piper on the estate of the Duke of Buccleuch at Dalkeith. He was paid a small retainer and was expected to entertain at all family occasions and to make a tour of the town twice a day at 5 a.m. and 8 p.m. He was given a special uniform each year, which comprised a long yellow coat with red lining, red plush breeches, white stockings and buckles for his shoes.

One of George's greatest admirers was Hugh Dalrymple, Lord Drummore. Himself a keen amateur performer, he once strolled out to the country dressed as a common piper. Along the way he met a glazier who offered him a dram and the friendly tradesman listened intently to the piping of the anonymous Lord. The glazier, commenting on his playing said, 'Foul fa' me, man, gin ye dinna play amaist as weel as our ain Geordie Syme.' The glazier had been on his way to clean Lord Drummore's windows and on arrival was pleasantly surprised to be given a glass of wine in return for his dram.

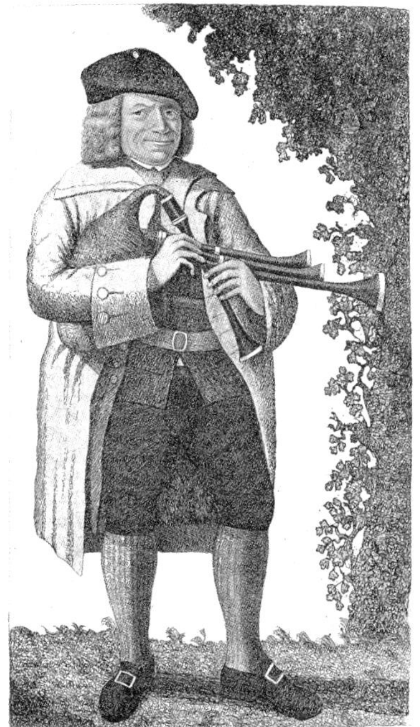

This represents old Geordy Sime
a Famous Piper in his time

Alexander Thomson and Miss Crawford
(no date)

A grocer in search of a wife

Alexander Thomson had many sobriquets. Having grown wealthy as a grocer, he was known as 'Prince of Grocers' but less complimentary was the title of 'Farthing Sandy', which referred to his issuing a great number of farthings 'for the better adjustment of accounts with his numerous customers'.

Realising that widowhood was not a desirable state, Thomson decided to pursue a connection with an aristocratic family. Kay shows him in hot pursuit of the elegant Miss Crawford, daughter of Sir Hew Crawford of Jordanhill, a scene witnessed by the artist on Calton Hill on the day that James Tytler (*III*) set off in his Great Edinburgh Fire Balloon from Holyrood. The grocer's quest was in vain and he duly became a subject of ridicule amongst the Edinburgh ladies. He also earned another sobriquet, 'Ruffles', which came from his habit of hiding his long hands underneath the ruffles of his sleeves.

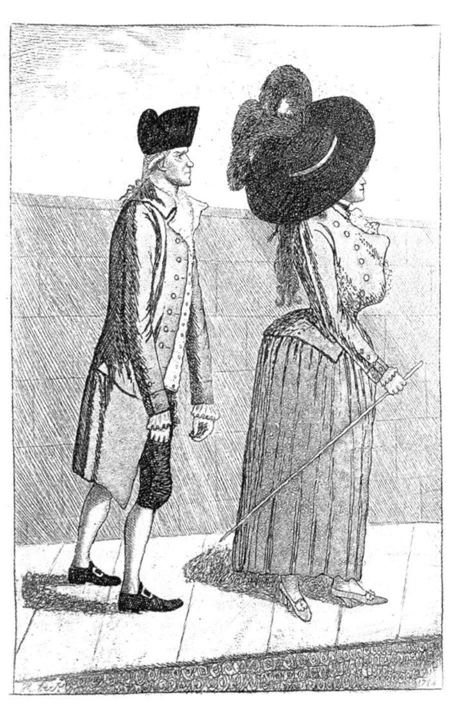

Three Legal Devotees, Andrew Nicol, Mary Walker and John Skene (1802)

In pursuit of justice

This is one of Kay's best etchings and is presented as a satire on judicial proceedings and the high hopes of the lower classes.

Andrew Nicol, or 'Muck Andrew' as he was known, decided to join the fashion for having a lawsuit and duly disputed the situation or boundary of a dunghill with a neighbour. The matter ended up in the Court of Session and 'Muck Andrew' is presented here, with his papers, on one of his weekly visits from his home in Kinross to get an update on his lawsuit. He was imprisoned for debt and died in jail in Cupar in 1817.

Mary Walker was known as a simpleton who walked about the Parliament Square in pursuit of monies she felt due to her from the Magistrates of Edinburgh.

John Skene, a flax dresser known as 'The Heckler', imagined himself to have two very influential roles in Edinburgh, first as Superintendent of the Court of Session and secondly as Superintendent of the General Assembly. He is seen here in clerical dress, ready to take 'imaginary' control of the deliberations of the Assembly and on one occasion almost persuaded Dr Blair to let him preach at the High Church.

Skene often declared that the clergy were much 'worse to keep in order than the lawyers'.

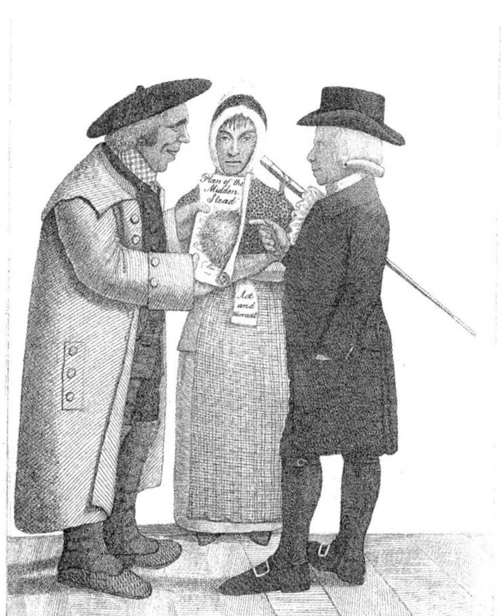

Plan of the Midden Stead
Act and Warrant
KAY 1792

Three Social Friends, Robert Kay, Louis Cauvin and David Scott (1817)

A walk in the country

Robert Kay (1740–1818), on the extreme left of the print, was a distant relative of the artist, who often visited him at his home in Duddingston. A builder and architect, Robert Kay prepared the scheme for the South Bridge in Edinburgh in 1785. Claimed to be the first urban viaduct of its kind in Europe, the final design was modified in the light of comments from Robert Adam, who had produced his own designs but which were considered too ornamental and too expensive. Kay also produced elevations for Charlotte Square in 1787 but on this occasion Robert Adam's designs of 1791 designs were accepted.

Louis Cauvin, in the centre, was a well-known teacher of French, with his most illustrious pupil being Robert Burns. He built Louisfield at the southeast corner of Duddingston, which was later converted to the Cauvin Hospital for the relief, maintenance and education of the sons of teachers, farmers, master-printers and booksellers. Cauvin had a great fear of body snatchers and left clear instructions that his corpse should be deposited in Restalrig Churchyard and 'watched over for a proper time'.

David Scott, to the right, was a farmer at Northfield in Edinburgh and an Elder of the historic parish church of Duddingston.

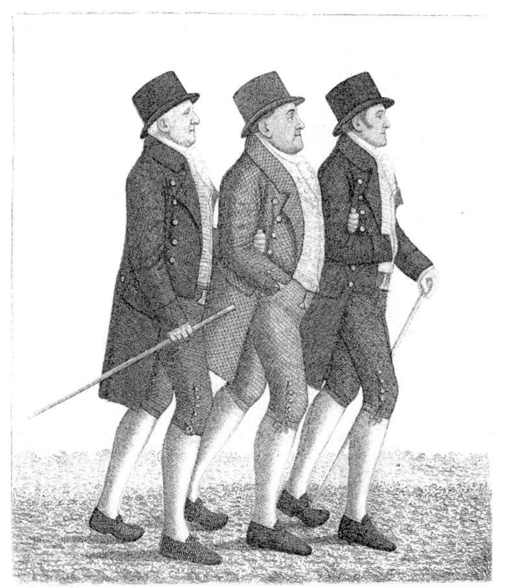

Voltaire, the French Philosopher and
Mr Watson, an Edinburgh Messenger (1789)

Seeing double

Kay's print highlights the remarkable resemblance of Mr Watson, a humble Messenger who lived in the Old Town of Edinburgh, with the great writer, essayist and philosopher, Voltaire. Kay copied this likeness of Voltaire from a snuff box that had belonged to John Davidson WS. The box had come from Paris and the likeness was considered to be a very good one.

Voltaire, whose real name was François-Marie Arouet, never visited Scotland but his acknowledgement of Scotland as a centre of intellect and genius is often quoted: 'We look to Scotland for all our ideas of civilisation.' Less frequently quoted is his comment on the joys of ice-cream: 'Ice-cream is exquisite – what a pity it isn't illegal.'

During Kay's lifetime the appearance in Edinburgh of several look-alikes is documented, one being Myles M'Phail (*III*) known locally as Lord North for his uncanny resemblance to the then Prime Minister and another, a visiting musician, who was deemed a double of Napoleon.

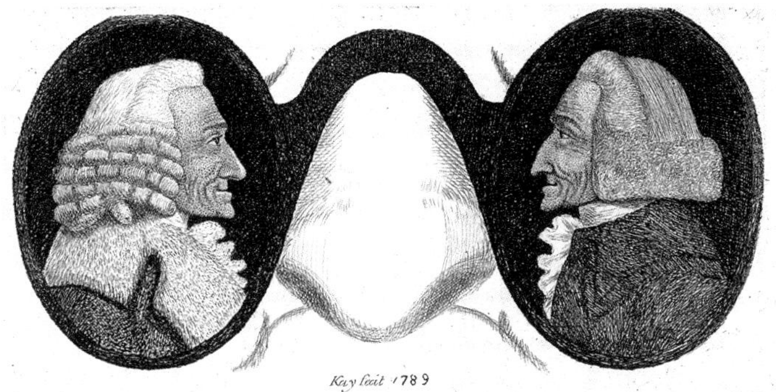

Kay fecit 1789

Alexander Wedderburn, Lord High Chancellor Loughborough, afterwards Earl of Rosslyn (1800)

The caustic statesman

Compared with the cruel caricatures of James Gillray and James Sayers, Kay's etching, completed during a short visit to London in 1800, is much kinder to his fellow countryman.

Alexander Wedderburn began his legal career in Edinburgh and in 1755 edited the first *Edinburgh Review,* whose supporters included his close friends Adam Smith (*LXXXVII*), William Robertson and David Hume. Two years later, after refusing to apologise for remarks made to a senior counsel, he informed the Bench, 'there is my gown, and I will never wear it more: *virtute me involve'* (I wrap myself in my integrity). He moved to London and rose through the ranks of the English Bar and Parliament to become in 1793 the first Scotsman to be made Lord Chancellor. He was given the titles of Lord Loughborough and later, in 1801, Earl of Rosslyn.

Noteworthy events in his life were winning an acquittal for Lord Clive, former Governor-General of India, on charges of 'undue appropriation' and in 1754 his hour-long rebuke of Benjamin Franklin for allegedly leaking letters written by Thomas Hutchinson, Governor of Massachusetts, in order to provoke unrest against the British Crown. The confrontation took place before the public and the Privy Council. Franklin remained silent throughout, with one observer describing his countenance as a picture of 'philosophic Tranquility and sovereign Contempt'.

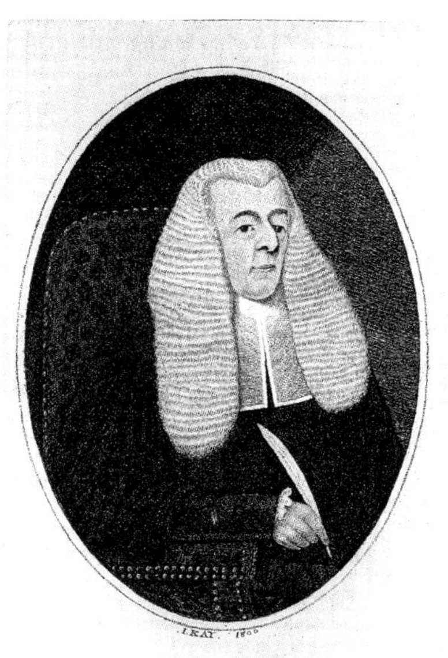
I. KAY. 1790

John Wemyss, Robert Clerk
and George Pratt (1784)

Caught between two town criers

Town crier John Wemyss was a colleague of the eccentric town crier, George Pratt. A dyer to trade, Wemyss was for many years officer to the Incorporation of Bonnet-makers, for which he was paid fifty shillings a year.

The central figure, Robert Clerk, was a bookseller and publisher in the Parliament Square, who latterly resided at Newhaven. It was said that there never existed 'a more honest and inoffensive man' but here the quiet gentleman is caught between two of the loudest men in the Old Town.

George Pratt was town-crier of Edinburgh around the year 1784, the date of Kay's print. Known for his pompous delivery, even the most commonplace announcements, such as the arrival of a fresh supply of skate, would be announced with as much gravitas as the birth of a new royal prince.

Despite Pratt's dedication to his public role, he was often teased by the local rogues, who would poke fun at his extensive double chin by referring publicly to his 'swallow's nest'.

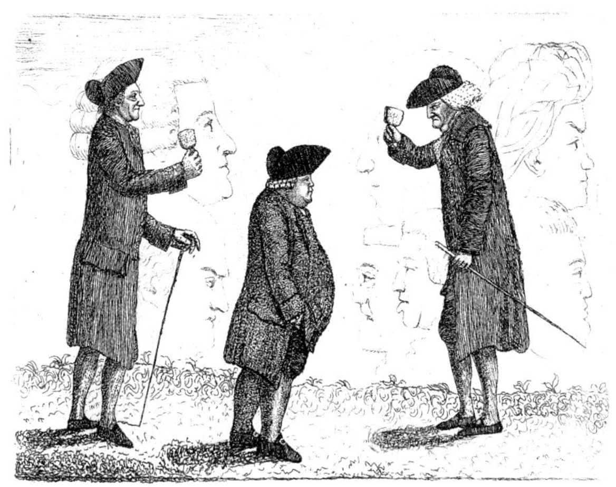

Rev. John Wesley, Dr Hamilton and the Rev. Mr Cole (1790)

A triumvirate of Methodists

Kay made this etching during Wesley's twenty-second and final visit to Edinburgh in 1790. The great Methodist is being supported on his left side by the Reverend Joseph Cole, then stationed in Edinburgh, and on the right side by Doctor James Hamilton, an active member of the Methodist Society in Scotland.

Wesley is said to have preached forty thousand sermons and travelled a quarter of a million miles in his lifetime. He considered the Scots quite different to the English and commented, 'Oh what a difference there is between South and North Britain – everyone here at least loves to hear the Word of God; and none takes it into his head to speak an uncivilised word to any for endeavours to save their souls.' But he also admitted that whilst his Scottish congregations were politely attentive, they also appeared to be unmoved by his message!

In Edinburgh, the Methodists were perceived by many as being 'largely English' while in Glasgow and the West the Wesleyan Methodists were to become an important part of the growth of Protestantism in a newly industrialising society. In Victorian Glasgow there were even enough churches to run a 'Wesleyan Sunday Football League!'

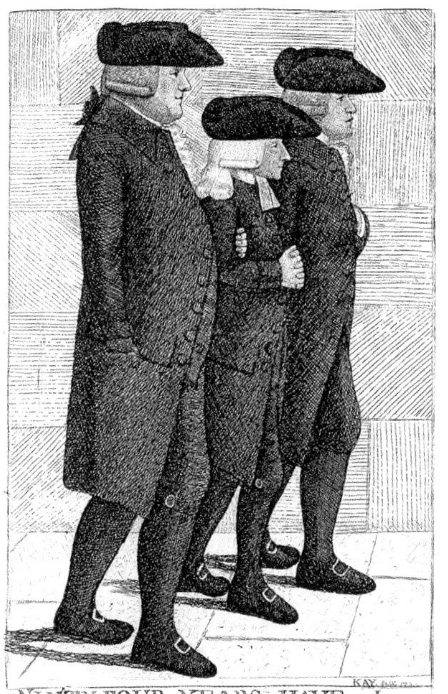

NINTY FOUR YEARS HAVE I
SOJOURNED UPON THIS EARTH
ENDEAVOURING TO DO GOOD

Ebenezer Wilson (1813)

The indolent bellman

Ebenezer Wilson became a member of the Incorporation of Hammermen in 1774 but was 'never remarkable for activity or enterprise'. When he petitioned the Incorporation for some money, pleading that he had neither work nor metal, one member observed dryly that Wilson would have little use for metal if he had no work!

He was appointed ringer of the Tron Kirk bell with a salary of £10 a year and often managed to escape the drudgery of ringing the bell himself by letting some of the High School lads 'jow the bell' at the appointed time of eight o'clock.

Johnnie Dowie's tavern was Ebenezer's regular howff and he was delighted to be the first to alert 'honest John' of the 'vintner's mortification' at the hand of Kay (*see XXVIII*). Ebenezer accompanied Dowie to make fun of his reaction to the print, only to find that Kay had committed his own likeness to paper and it was posted side by side with the vintner. In disgust, Ebenezer discarded his apron, hoping to make the portrait less characteristic but he still retained his old-fashioned cocked hat and shoe buckles.

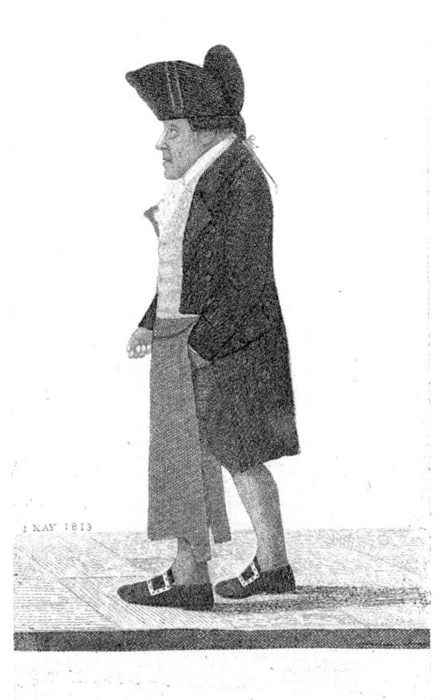

J. KAY 1813

Alexander Wood, Surgeon (1784)

A smooth operator

Alexander Wood, known as Lang Sandy Wood on account of his tall, lanky appearance, was a most revered surgeon, placed by his pupil, John Bell, 'to the first rank in a most useful profession'.

He was one of many skilled operators at the Royal Infirmary and his 'celebrity' patients included James Boswell and Robert Burns. Lang Sandy was a subscriber to the first Edinburgh edition of Burns's poems and his written commendation helped to secure Burns' appointment as Commissioner of Excise.

According to Henry Mackenzie, Lang Sandy was the first to use an umbrella around 1780 and he was also known for his eccentric habit of keeping a pet raven that often accompanied him on his visits to patients.

Sandy bore a striking resemblance to Sir James Stirling (*XXXI*), the Lord Provost of Edinburgh. Once, when attacked by a group of youths who thought they had the unpopular Provost in their grasp, he begged them with the words, 'I'm lang Sandy Wood – tak' me to a lamp and ye'll see.'

He was a founder member of the Aesculapian Club in 1773 and treasured his Diploma of 'Doctor of Mirth' awarded to him by the members in 1803. Mirth and Bacchus sometimes got the better of Sandy and his good friend, Dr Andrew Duncan (*XXX*), once had to explain his absence thus:

Shed no tears, my good Friends,
wear no garments of sable
Sandy Wood is not dead but laid under the table!

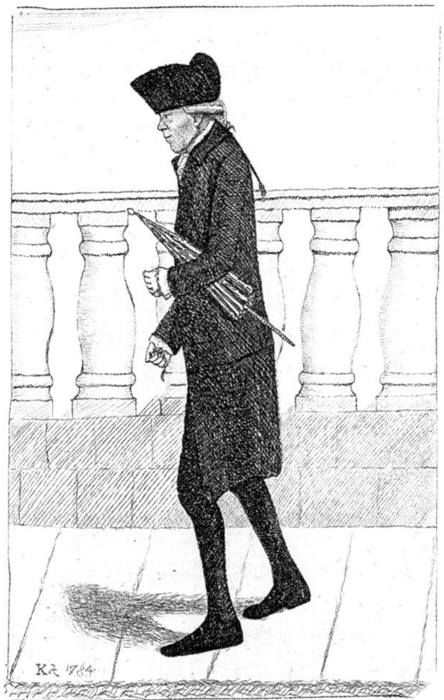

ILLUSTRATION BY
JOSEF SZATKOWSKI